# A Guide to Feminist
# Family Therapy

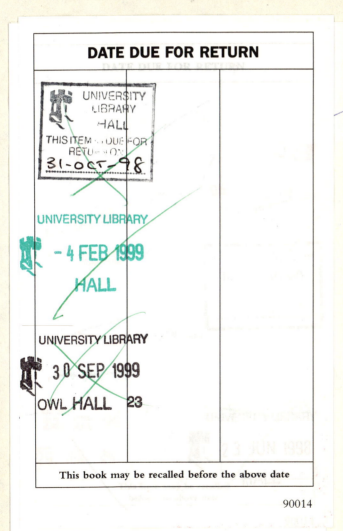

# A Guide to Feminist Family Therapy

### Edited by
### Lois Braverman

*A Guide to Feminist Family Therapy* was simultaneously issued by The Haworth Press, Inc. under the title *Women, Feminism and Family Therapy*, a special issue of *Journal of Psychotherapy & the Family*, Volume 3, Number 4, Winter 1987, Lois Braverman, Guest Editor.

Harrington Park Press
New York • London

ISBN 0-918393-48-5

Published by

Harrington Park Press, Inc., 12 West 32 Street, New York, New York 10001
EUROSPAN/Harrington, 3 Henrietta Street, London WC2E 8LU England

Harrington Park Press, Inc. is a subsidiary of The Haworth Press, Inc., 12 West 32 Street, New York, New York 10001.

*A Guide to Feminist Family Therapy* was originally published as *Journal of Psychotherapy & the Family*, Volume 3, Number 4, Winter 1987.

Cover design by Marshall Andrews.

**LIBRARY OF CONGRESS**
**Library of Congress Cataloging-in-Publication Data**

A Guide to feminist therapy / edited by Lois Braverman.
    p. cm.
    "Simultaneously issued by The Haworth Press, Inc. under the title Women, feminism and family therapy, a special issue of Journal of psychotherapy & the family, volume 3, number 4, Winter 1987, Lois Braverman, guest editor."
    Includes bibliographical references.
    ISBN 0-918393-48-5
    1. Feminist therapy. 2. Family psychotherapy. I. Braverman. Lois.
RC489.F45G85 1988
616.89' 156—dc 19                                87-35180
                                                      CIP

## DEDICATION

This book is dedicated to
my grandmother Becky Hoffman (1894-1977)
and to her namesake
Benjamin John Braverman-Scult (born February 5, 1987)

## ABOUT THE EDITOR

**Lois Braverman, ACSW,** directs the Des Moines Family Therapy Institute and maintains an extensive private practice. In her publications and conference presentations she has critically examined the assumptions implicit in the major schools of family therapy about women's role in the family, in the workplace, and in the psychotherapeutic setting. Ms. Braverman continues to pursue her interest in the relationship between feminism and family therapy through her editorship of the new *Journal of Feminist Family Therapy* and her work as a consultant to numerous public and private organizations. Her video "A Feminist Perspective" has been published by the Menninger Foundation. She lives with her husband and two sons, ages 8 years and 10 months, in Des Moines, Iowa.

# CONTENTS

# EDITORIAL NOTE

I am especially delighted that the *Journal of Psychotherapy & the Family* is devoting a special issue focusing on "Women, Feminism and Family Therapy." It has been my intention from the start of this Journal that such an issue would be published. The Journal is dedicated to improving the arts and sciences of psychotherapy practice by focusing on the family and its role in the prevention, development and maintenance of psychopathology.

The aim of the Journal is to provide the most well-written, accurate, authoritative, and relevant information on critical issues in the practice of psychotherapy with families. We hope that this issue, consistent with the Journal's aim, will promote new insight among psychotherapy students and practitioners into the nature and special role of women and feminist thinking applied to family therapy.

There is always the chance that readers—particularly males—may be repulsed by a special issue focusing on women and feminist psychotherapy with what appears to be a rather narrow set of objectives. I am certain, however, that Journal subscribers and other readers will be pleased with this collection. The reason why this issue is so important to the field of psychotherapy is, in part, its controversial nature. For feminism and its application to psychotherapy calls into question the basic assumptions of the work of psychotherapy: that men and women are not equal; that we live in a basically patriarchal culture; and that marriage is a political institution which, from the wedding day on, structurally limits the resources and choices of wives in comparison with their husbands.

We assume that there are benefits to recognizing the status quo, the inferior *status* of women and the social and interpersonal factors which maintain this status. Moreover, psychotherapists, equipped with a more feminist-sensitive perspective and specific strategies for validating women's realities, women's interpretations, and women's contributions, will be more sensitive human beings.

Yet this special issue of the Journal goes beyond promoting sensitivity. Specifically, the issue contributes to the family psychotherapy literature by (1) providing an update of the continuing theoretical development of feminist family therapy, (2) applying a feminist-sensitive perspective in the treatment of women, and (3) discussing the implications of feminist-sensitive perspective to psychotherapy training and supervision, particularly family therapy. It is an important achievement that required considerable dedication and hard work by the thirteen contributing scholars. These women and men represent several disciplines, theoretical approaches, and areas of expertise. The task of editing this special issue of the Journal, of organizing and coordinating such diverse people and works, required a mastery of both diplomacy and scholarly literatures.

Lois Braverman, the Editor of "Women, Feminism and Family Therapy," is a nationally recognized feminist and psychotherapist who has been extremely active in efforts to expand the feminist and psychotherapy literatures, particularly in social work and family therapy. She is Director and co-founder of the Des Moines Family Therapy Institute. She is former Director of the Des Moines Educational Center and Assistant Professor of the University of Iowa School of Social Work. Her publications and national presentations have challenged assumptions implicit in major schools of family therapy about women's role in the family, the work place, and the psychotherapeutic setting. Her video "A Feminist Perspective," has been published by the Menninger Foundation and is being nationally circulated.

With her contributions and national reputation, it is not surprising that she was able to assemble such an excellent collection of papers written by nationally known scholar clinicians. Judith Myers Avis, a professor of family therapy at the University of Guelph is one of the most respected contributors in this area and here provides a useful historical overview of feminism and its impact on family therapy.

Harriet Goldhor Lerner, of the Menninger Foundation, is a well-known scholar and author of the highly acclaimed *The Dance of Anger* (Harper and Row, 1985). She is a noted author on the psychology of women who, in addition to publishing in professional journals, has published in popular magazines such as *Ms. Magazine*, *Working Mother*, *Cosmopolitan*, and *Nation's Business*.

Michele Bograd, a Cambridge clinical psychologist with a faculty appointment at Harvard University, is well-published in feminist psychological literature as well as a frequent contributor to *Family Therapy Networker*. She is most noted for her early analysis of the failings of family systems theory in the analysis of wife abuse.

Margaret Cotroneo, a professor and Program Director of Psychiatric-Mental Health Nursing, at the University of Pennsylvania, has made important contributions to both family therapy and feminist psychotherapy, specifically on the topics of contextual family therapy, families and abuse, family decision-making in child custody disputes and applied ethics.

Claudia Bepko is co-director of the Family Therapy Associates of Fair Haven, New Jersey. She is a noted expert in the area of treatment of alcoholic systems. She is author with Jo-Ann Krestan of *The Responsibility Trap* (MacMillan Free Press, 1985).

Jo-Ann Krestan is director of Family Therapy Associates of Fair Haven, NJ. Her clinical expertise is well recognized in the field of family therapy. For example, she has been invited as a Master Therapist to the AAMFT 1987 Conference. She is author (with Claudia Bepko) of the first article on treatment with lesbian couples published by *Family Process* in 1980.

Richard C. Schwartz is a professor at the University of Illinois, Chicago and Coordinator of Training and Research at the Family Systems Program, Institute for Juvenile Research in Chicago. Mary Jo Barrett is Director of Midwest Family Resource in Chicago and co-editor of another important special issue of the Journal (Volume 2:2, *Treating Incest: A Multiple Systems Perspective*).

Linda Webb-Watson (Woodard) is a family therapist with the Dallas Salesmanship Club's Youth and Family Centers, Inc., and has a private practice in Dallas, Texas. She teaches family therapy at the graduate level and in a training institute. Her interests include systemic applications in larger systems, ethnicity and its implications in therapy and systemic therapy with families with medical problems.

Ann Hartman is a leader is applying a family systems perspective to the issues of child welfare as reflected in her most recent book *Working with Adoptive Families: Beyond Placement* (Child Welfare League of America, 1984). She is co-founder of the Ann Arbor Center for the Family and is currently the Dean of the Smith College of Social Work. Her most well-known book is Family Centered Social Work Practice (Free Press, 1983).

Joan Laird, co-founder of the Ann Arbor Center for the Family, is a figure of influence in both family therapy and social work fields. Her most recent book (co-edited with Ann Hartman) is *A Handbook of Child Welfare: Context, Knowledge and Process* (Free Press, 1985). She is most noted in the family therapy field for her thoughtfulness regarding family myths and ritual. She and Ann Hartman were plenary speakers at the 1987 AFTA Meeting in Chicago on this Topic.

Marianne Ault-Riché is Curriculum Coordinator of the Marriage and Family Therapy Program of the Menninger Foundation. The Program focuses on an Integrated Model of family therapy, combining structural, strategic, interaction, systemic, behavior, object relations, and multi-generational approaches. This model is described in her book (with co-author David Rosenthal), *Family Therapy for a New Age: Seeing Through Techniques and Integrating Models* (Prentice Hall, 1987). She is also editor of *Women and Family Therapy* (Aspen, 1986), the first known book on women and family therapy.

This collection completes the third volume of the Journal: three years of publications of useful resource texts for practicing psychotherapists. As Editor of the Journal, I hope that readers continue to find these collections relevant and innovative. I hope that you will write me at Purdue (525 Russell Street, W. Lafayette, IN 47906) with your comments and suggestions.

*Charles R. Figley, PhD*
*Editor*

## Feminism and Family Therapy:
## Friends or Foes

### Lois Braverman

Recent family therapy literature demonstrates growing concern and attention to feminist and women's issues; clinicians are examining family therapy models for biases against women and questioning whether feminist and family systems perspectives can be integrated. On the level of theory, important pioneering work by Virginia Goldner (1985a; 1985b) and Judith Libow et al. (1982) has begun to chart the problems involved in integrating the concepts of family therapy with a feminist perspective. A feminist perspective requires that we commit ourselves to resolving those difficulties and resist the temptation to operate as if our theories and practices were gender-blind. Goldner (1986) insists that we must put gender, as a unit of analysis, on the same level of importance as generation. In the area of clinical application, the collection by Ault-Riché (1986) and the case studies in *The Family Therapy Networker* (Simon, 1985) have begun to operationalize Goldner's prescription.

The objectives of this issue are to: (1) continue the theoretical discussion through a critique of family therapy concepts from a

Lois Braverman, ACSW, is currently the Director of the Des Moines Family Therapy Institute and maintains a private practice. Correspondence may be addressed to 3833 Woods Drive, Des Moines, IA 50312.

feminist perspective; (2) apply a feminist-sensitive perspective to treatment issues peculiar to women; and finally (3) to explore the implications of a feminist approach to training and supervision in family therapy.

The question which comes to mind as we put together this special issue is simply, "What has taken us so long?" Feminist issues have been avoided by family therapists as emotionally loaded and threatening to the way we look at things and conceptualize them. As long as we thought systemically and did not buy into a traditional linear long-term psychodynamic approach to treatment, we considered ourselves to be far ahead of other helping professionals. So while other therapeutic frameworks and treatment modalities of the 1970s were marked by feminist critiques (Chesler, 1972; Franks & Burtle, 1974; Cox, 1976; Miller, 1976; Blum, 1977; Rawlings & Carter, 1977; Chodorow, 1978) which questioned traditional psychodynamic theory and practice, we, as family therapists, had our heads buried in the sand.[1] We were absorbed in the "systemically righteous" endeavors of treating families, seeing symptoms contextually, and defending the legitimacy of our treatment models.

Now that we are ready to pull our heads out of the sand, we confront more directly the implications of looking at our concepts and practices from a feminist perspective: a feminist critique shakes the very precepts upon which our epistemology is based; it challenges the notion that men and women are equal participants in the relational dance; it challenges the idea that there is no villain and no victim. A feminist perspective demands that we take seriously the consequences of living in a patriarchal culture: marriage is not just an interactional scene, but a political institution reflective of the patriarchal culture in which it is immersed. Who compromises more of self is determined by the political nature of marriage. Women enter the family arena with less access to economic resources and advancement, with less visibility and power in policymaking positions in both private and public spheres. A feminist-informed practice takes seriously the notion that "the personal is political" — that, for example, married women's high rates of depression may well be connected to their sex role, sociocultural legacy (Miller, 1976; Braverman, 1986c), and powerlessness in the marital arena (Braverman, 1986b). A feminist critique leads us to question what we consider to be "normal family processes" and "significant life cycle events." For example, the onset of female menstruation has been noticeably absent from the literature as a significant force which reorganizes relationships in the family system (Braverman, 1986b).

Institutionally, a feminist perspective insists that we examine the complexities and subtleties of the use of sexist language in our journals, our conference presentations, and our books, as well as the painful issue of who gets included and who gets excluded from our professional areas of prestige and power, our editorial boards, our university faculties, and our organizational boards of directors (for a beginning effort of this sort see Avis, 1985 & Braverman, 1986d). We might note that in the recounting of the history of the family therapy movement, the contributions of women, most notably social workers of the 1920s and 1930s, are often overlooked (Broderick & Schrader, 1981; Braverman, 1986a). As Judith Libow (1985, p. 37) notes, "Social workers such as Mary Richmond and Charlotte Towle were among the earliest pioneers advocating the importance of working with individuals in the context of the family even prior to World War I, yet are given little credit for their actual contribution."

Looking outside our own discipline of marriage and family therapy, we find evidence of this same "benign neglect." Feminist scholars in the history of science (Evelyn Fox Keller, 1985) have documented the seeming invisibility of women in the discovery and development of paradigms in the natural sciences and have begun to bring the significant advances made by women scientists to light as well as to examine the difficulties these women faced in bringing their work into the scientific mainstream. During the last decade they have attempted what one may call a "radical critique of science" by questioning the assumptions of scientific knowledge, most notably its notions of what is objective, neutral, and universal. Anne Fausto-Sterling (1985) in her profound study, *Myths of Gender*, demonstrates how the very construction of sociobiological and genetic theories about the differences between men and women and abilities of girls and boys are in fact quite colored by social and political beliefs. The very nature of many of the scientific questions asked reflects their basis in a patriarchally influenced world view.

This examination of the "invisibility of women" in the sciences finds an echo in history, philosophy, and linguistics as well. In her review of the recent literature on women's language Fern Johnson (1986, p. 318) puts the challenge eloquently:

. . . coming to terms with women's language is literally the challenge to put the nature of language to the test—to recognize its power to name the world, to enter the creative realm implied in knowing that language and thought, language and society, language and culture all work reciprocally on one another to construct the interiors of self and private relationships, and the exteriors of social structures, processes and institutions.

I would suggest that feminism and family therapy have much to offer one another—they are not essentially incongruent. Techniques such as reframing, positive connotation, unbalancing, enactment, sculpting, and paradoxical prescriptions are not in and of themselves sexist or inherently oppressive to the female client—mothers and wives in particular. In fact, I would argue that the techniques of the major schools of family therapy—multigenerational, strategic, structural, and systemic—lend themselves particularly well to resolving many of the clinical problems of women. The problem, then, is not the technique, but the values of the therapist employing it—his or her sensitivities to the feminist perspective. Burke's (1982) research supports this view by showing that the values of the therapist, not his or her technique, determine whether or not their therapeutic practices are sexist. The following is a beginning attempt to formulate the considerations which would underlie a feminist-sensitive approach to treatment, whatever the particular technique being employed. Such considerations might include:

1. understanding the impact of a patriarchal system on both men and women, and acknowledging that the social and political contexts (e.g., lower salaries for women, numerical scarcity of women in positions of power, etc.), as well as the family context, have a significant influence on the problems of women.
2. recognizing the limitations of traditional theories of psychological development based on a male model of maturity.
3. familiarity with women's problem-solving processes which tend to focus on connection and relationship, rather than on logic, abstraction, and rationality.
4. understanding that the "personal is political," that is: motherhood, childrearing, and marriage are not simply life-cycle

events, but institutions that carry particular sociocultural legacies for women.
5. a sensitivity to the biological effects of the female life cycle
(including menstruation, adolescence, pregnancy, childbirth,
and menopause) on women's symptom presentation and interpersonal relationships.
6. understanding women's sexuality and sexual responsiveness
so that confused and mistaken notions, such as the exclusivity
of vaginal orgasm, are not perpetuated.
7. valuing women's relationships with each other as a special
source of support, different from their relationships with men.[2]

On the level of theory, a feminist approach to family therapy,
whatever the school, requires embracing gender as a critical vari-
able in the formulation of problem definition and problem solution.
In practice it requires the therapist to ask how a feminist perspective
influences the formulation of hypotheses, treatment goals, and the
conduct of therapist-client interactions, especially where the emphasis and responsibility for change is put.

## *PREVIEW OF THE CONTENTS*

This collection of essays includes papers written by scholars from
a variety of mental health disciplines. All the authors are practicing
psychotherapists who have struggled with the problems of integrating a feminist perspective with the practice of family therapy. The
collection is divided into three sections dealing with theoretical issues, clinical applications, and supervision and training issues re-
spectively.

The collection is introduced by Judith Myers Avis's historical
review of the literature which has attempted to integrate feminist
issues and family therapy. Professor Avis's article "Deepening
Awareness: A Private Study Guide to Feminism and Family Therapy" provides the practicing psychotherapist with a marvelously
complete, annotated bibliography on feminist theory and frameworks, research on sex differences, as well as a summary of the
research on women and mental health, and works which present a
feminist critique of family therapy. In addition to the fullness of her
summary, I believe that Professor Avis guides her readers well
through this relatively "uncharted territory."

Harriet Goldhor Lerner challenges the strength of Bowen Family

Systems Theory as a model of treatment for women in her article "Is Family Systems Theory Really Systemic? A Feminist Communication." Although she personally finds it to be the theory most congruent with her feminist values and practices, she argues that family context alone is not broad enough for analysis and neglects the patriarchal culture in which both women and men live.

Michele Bograd's essay "Enmeshment, Fusion or Relatedness? A Conceptual Analysis" questions the language of family therapy applying a feminist linguistic analysis to the terms "enmeshment" and "fusion." The issues of women's language and a feminist critique of other linguistic formulations has been sorely neglected among family therapists, though it has occurred in other disciplines (Daly, 1978; Thorne, Kramarae & Henley, 1983; Frank & Anshen, 1983; Kramarae & Treichler, 1985). Bograd argues that the concepts of enmeshment and fusion are based on a male model of transaction and so tend to lead to women's transactional styles being pathologized. She challenges the field to develop concepts that positively describe women's capacity for attachments as well as men's capacity for separation.

The issues of abuse have been identified in the literature as particularly important for women. Since publication of Lenore Walker's *The Battered Women* (1979) the abuse of women and particularly of wives has been cited as one of the most extreme examples of the notion that women are the property of husbands and subject to their whims and desires. For years police and law enforcement agencies have not seriously involved themselves in protecting women from the consequences of domestic violence. To those psychotherapists who treated women in violent relationships, particularly those who worked with women in the late 70s and early 80s in family violence shelters, family therapy, with its systemic notions of mutual reciprocity and no villain or victim, were unacceptable models of treatment. Certainly the issue of abuse of women is one example of "the personal is political" in rarified form. Margaret Cotroneo in her article, "Women and Abuse in the Context of the Family," demonstrates how the use of contextual family therapy is a useful model of treatment for abused women and continues the pioneering work of Michele Bograd (1984) in this area.

Claudia Bepko in her essay, "Female Legacies: Intergenerational Themes and Their Treatment for Women in Alcoholic Families," provides the reader with an enlightening perspective on the parallel dilemmas of both alcoholic women, and women functioning in a family system with another alcoholic member, either parents or spouse. Using Bowen Family Systems Theory as the treatment model, Bepko argues that the acknowledgment of gender differences is essential to the treatment of women in alcoholic systems.

In a culture that Adrienne Rich (1980) has described as "compulsively heterosexual," Jo-Ann Krestan in her article "Lesbian Daughters and Lesbian Mothers: The Crisis of Disclosure from a Family Systems Perspective," examines the difficulties that women face in disclosing their lesbianism to their mothers, and that lesbian mothers who "come out" confront with their daughters. Bowen family systems theory is the family therapy model used to coach lesbian women involved in the coming out process. This article shifts the focus from the issues of difference (Krestan & Bepko, 1980; Roth, 1985) between the lesbian couple and their heterosexual counterparts (previously the sole focus of the family therapy literature) to the neglected area of mother-daughter disclosure in the coming out process.

Richard C. Schwartz and Mary Jo Barrett's article "Women and Eating Disorders" demonstrates a model of treatment that includes an emphasis on both the family and individual process for the treatment of bulimia and anorexia. Eating disorders are most prevalent among women and a full appreciation of the sociocultural message to women to "be thin" is essential to the therapist's analysis of the problem.

Linda Webb-Watson's essay, "Women, Family Therapy, and Larger Systems," demonstrates how the family therapist has to consider and treat often not just the family, but more importantly the "politics" of the referring system which might involve sexist and racist notions bearing quite heavily upon the problem. Using a systemic model of family therapy, the author, in her case example, artfully guides the referring system, with strong prejudices against African-American single parent families, to a new view of the problem and its solution.

Joan Laird and Ann Hartman's article, "Women, Rituals, and Family Therapy," takes us on a different journey, examining the role of ritual in women's public and private lives. Their feminist analysis of women's rituals in their families offers the reader clinical examples of how women's experience might be expanded and transformed through the use of ritual.

The collection concludes with Marianne Ault-Riché's essay "Teaching an Integrated Model of Family Therapy: Women as Students, Women as Supervisors.'' She provides the reader with rich case examples for both training and supervision using a Feminist-Informed Integrated Model of family therapy. The issues of feminist-informed training and supervision are essential to both sensitizing family therapists to the issues of women and sexism and to the development of new ways of understanding and treating women and their families.

## ACKNOWLEDGMENTS

I want to thank all the contributors for helping me put together what I think has turned out to be, due to their efforts, a significant volume in the feminist family therapy literature. In addition to the editorial board, I wish to acknowledge the following people who served as outside referees: Virginia Goldner, Paul Lambakis, and Marilyn Mason. Special thanks go to Charles Figley and Froma Walsh for their support and encouragement in initiating this project. Finally, a personal note of thanks to my husband, Allen Scult, for being an important consulting colleague, supportive friend and nurturing cook who fed me emotionally and physically through the birth of our second son and the birth of this book.

## NOTES

1. The exception to this, of course, is Rachel Hare-Mustin's (1978) early critique of family therapy.

2. This list is adapted from an earlier version published by the author (Braverman, 1986b, p. 90-101).

## REFERENCES

Ault-Riché, M. (Ed.) (1986). *Women and Family Therapy*. Rockville, MD: Aspen Systems Corporation.

Avis, J.M. (1985). The Politics of Functional Family Therapy: A Feminist Critique. *Journal of Marital and Family Therapy, 11*, 127-138.

Blum, H.P. (Ed.) (1977). *Female Psychology: Contemporary Psychoanalytic Views*. New York: International Universities Press.

Bograd, M. (1984). Family Systems Approaches to Wife Battering: A Feminist Critique. *American Journal of Orthopsychiatry, 54*, 559-563.

Braverman, L. (1986a). Social Casework and Strategic Therapy. *Social Casework: The Journal of Contemporary Social Work, 67*, 234-239.

Braverman, L. (1986b). The Depressed Women in Context: A Feminist Family

Therapist's Analysis. In M. Ault-Riché (Ed.), *Women and Family Therapy*. Rockville, MD: Aspen Systems, 90-101.

Braverman, L. (1986c). Reframing the Female Client's Profile. *Affilia: Journal of Women and Social Work, 1*, 30-40.

Braverman, L. (1986d). Beyond Families: Strategic Family Therapy and the Female Client. *Family Therapy, 13*, 143-152.

Broderick, C.B. & Schrader, S.S. (1981). The History of Professional Marriage and Family Therapy. In A.S. Gurman and D.P. Kniskern (Eds.), *Handbook of Family Therapy*. New York: Brunner Mazel.

Burke, J. (1982). Suggestions for a Sex-Fair Curriculum in Family Treatment. *Journal of Education for Social Work, 18*, 98-102.

Chesler, P. (1972). *Women and Madness*. Garden City, NY: Doubleday.

Chodorow, N. (1978). *The Reproduction of Mothering: Psychoanalysis and the Sociology of Gender*. Berkeley: University of California Press.

Cox, S. (Ed.) (1976). *Female Psychology: The Emerging Self*. Chicago: Science Research Associates.

Daly, M. (1978). *Gyn/Ecology: The Metaethics of Radical Feminism*. Boston: Beacon Press.

Fausto-Sterling, A. (1985). *Myths of Gender: Biological Theories About Men and Women*. New York: Basic Books Publishers.

Frank, F. & Anshen, F. (1983). *Language and the Sexes*. Albany: SUNY Press.

Franks, V. & Burtle, V. (Eds.) (1974). *Women in Therapy*. New York: Brunner Mazel.

Goldner, V. (1985a). Feminism and Family Therapy. *Family Process, 24*, 31-47.

Goldner, V. (1985b). Warning: Family Therapy May Be Dangerous to Your Health. *The Family Therapy Networker, 9*, 19-23.

Goldner, V. (1986). Gender and the Politics of Family Therapy: Some Recent Thoughts. Presentation at the Eighth Annual Meeting of the American Family Therapy Association, June 18-22, Washington, D.C.

Hare-Mustin, R.T. (1978). A Feminist Approach to Family Therapy. *Family Process, 17*, 181-194.

Johnson, F.L. (1986). Coming to Terms with Women's Language. *The Quarterly Journal of Speech, 72*, 318-330.

Kramarae, C. & Treichler, P.A. (1985). *A Feminist Dictionary*. Boston: Pandora.

Keller, E.F. (1985). *Reflections on Gender and Science*. New Haven: Yale University Press.

Krestan, J. & Bepko, C. (1980). The Problem of Fusion in the Lesbian Relationship. *Family Process, 19*, 277-289.

Libow, J.A., Raskin, P.A. & Caust, B.L. (1982). Feminist and Family Systems Therapy: Are They Irreconcilable? *The American Journal of Family Therapy, 10*, 3-12.

Libow, J. (1985). Gender and Sex Role Issues as Family Secrets. *Journal of Strategic and Systemic Therapies, 4*, 32-41.

Miller, J.B. (1976). *Toward a New Psychology of Women*. Boston: Beacon Press.

Rawlings, E. & Carter, D. (1977). *Psychotherapy for Women*. Springfield, IL: Charles C. Thomas Publishers.

Rich, A. (1980). Compulsory Heterosexuality and Lesbian Existence. *Signs: Journal of Women in Culture and Society, 5*, 631-660.

Roth, S. (1985). Psychotherapy with Lesbian Couples: Individual Issues, Female

Socialization, and the Social Context. *Journal of Marital and Family Therapy,* *11*, 273-286.

Simon, R. (Ed.) (1985). Feminism: Shedding New Light on the Family. *Family Therapy Networker, 9*(6).

Thorne, B., Kramarae, C. & Henley, N. (Eds.) (1983). *Language, Gender, and Society*. Rowley, MA: Newbury House.

Walker, L. (1979). *The Battered Women*. New York: Harper Colophon Books.

# Deepening Awareness:
# A Private Study Guide
# to Feminism and Family Therapy

Judith Myers Avis

**SUMMARY.** This article provides an overview and annotated reading guide to feminist issues in family therapy and related disciplines. Six different areas of feminist theorizing and research are discussed, beginning with a fairly extensive overview of the feminist critique in family therapy. This is followed by discussions of feminist theory and frameworks, the feminist critique of the family, research on sex differences, research on women and mental health, and contemporary research and theory on women's development. For each area, the major issues emerging from the literature are summarized and a list of annotated key readings is provided.

The purpose of this article is to provide an overview, reference, and reading guide to feminist issues in family therapy. Five years ago it could not have been written—there *was* no feminist literature in family therapy, with the exception of several pioneering efforts (Hare-Mustin, 1978, 1979, 1980; Caust, Libow & Raskin, 1981), and the women's movement had had no visible impact on the field. In the ensuing years a growing feminist voice has been heard in family therapy, expressed in more than 30 articles and books. This work is grounded in the massive research and literature on women produced in other disciplines during the late 1960s and 1970s, a literature which can be daunting to those just beginning to explore it. Based on the assumption that most active clinicians have limited time for reading, this guide is designed to provide an overview of major issues and themes emerging from the feminist literature in

Judith Myers Avis, PhD, is Associate Professor in the Department of Family Studies at the University of Guelph, Guelph, Ontario, Canada N1G 2W1.

*15*

family therapy and in other related fields, as well as an annotated list of readings for further study.

The material is organized in two main sections. In the first, six different areas of feminist theorizing and research are discussed, beginning with a fairly extensive overview of the feminist critique of family therapy. This overview is followed by discussions of feminist theory and frameworks, the feminist critique of the family, research on sex differences, research and literature on women's mental health, and contemporary research and theory on women's development. The second section provides annotations of key readings for each of these areas. Although all of the areas discussed overlap and are related to each other, they are discussed separately for purposes of clarity and organization. The feminist critique of family therapy is discussed first to establish a framework for the rest of the article.

## THE FEMINIST CRITIQUE
## OF FAMILY THERAPY

### Isolation from Contemporary Theory and Research Concerning Women

A recurring theme in the feminist critique of family therapy is the isolation of the field from contemporary theory and research in other disciplines concerning women (Avis, 1985a; Caust, Libow & Raskin, 1981; Goldner, 1985a; James & McIntyre, 1983; Lerner, 1987). Various reasons have been suggested for family therapy's failure to respond to or incorporate the literature on women, including the dominance of family therapy by male leaders, the awkward questions the feminist critique raises regarding the viability of the family and of family therapy itself, and the possibility that family therapists believe they are already practicing in a nonsexist, nonblaming way which incorporates the major concerns of the women's movement (James & McIntyre, 1983).

However, the fundamental factor cited by most authors as primarily responsible for the field's isolation is family therapy's commitment to and reliance upon systems theory as the single organizing framework for conceptualizing and intervening in family relationships. This is a central theme in the feminist critique of family therapy.

## The Inadequacy of Systemic Formulations
## of Family Dysfunction

In spite of its early promise for providing a powerful and apparently nonblaming means of intervening in family problems, family systems theory has come under severe attack by feminist writers who argue that viewing families through a systems theory lens has critical consequences for how family therapists see women and their problems. Couched in the abstract, neutral language of cybernetics, family systems theory likens the family to a machine and reduces family functioning to what James and McIntyre (1983) call "a special case of a system" (p. 122), which functions according to specific systemic rules and is divorced from its historical, social, economic, and political contexts. By viewing the family out of context, family therapists locate family dysfunction entirely within interpersonal relationships in the family, ignore broader patterns of dysfunction occurring across families, and fail to notice the relationship between social context and family dysfunction (James & McIntyre, 1983; Lerner, 1987). By taking the family out of its historical context, systems theory also blinds us to the historical roots of the family, including the impact of the industrial revolution on contemporary family structure and the gendered division of labor. Systems theory does not even allow us to raise questions concerning the causality of family dysfunction since it is a theory of problem maintenance, not of causation (James & McIntyre, 1983; Taggart, 1985).

Feminists also find problematic the systemic concepts of circularity, neutrality, and complementarity. Notions of circularity imply that members engage in a never-ending, repetitive pattern of mutually reinforcing behaviors and are regarded by feminists as looking "suspiciously like a hypersophisticated version of blaming the victim and rationalizing the status quo" (Goldner, 1985a, p. 33). When applied to problems such as battering, rape, and incest, circular causality subtly removes responsibility for his behavior from the man while implying that the woman is coresponsible, and in some ways plays into the interactional pattern which results in violence and abuse (Bograd, 1984).

Similarly, systemic notions of neutrality emphasize that all parts of the system contribute *equally* to the production and maintenance of problems/dysfunction, and render totally invisible differences in power and influence between different family members. They also cause questions of individual rights and responsibility to disappear (Taggart, 1985). Further, concepts of sex roles and complementarity "obscure aspects of power and domination by appealing to the prettier, democratic construct of 'separate but equal'" (Goldner, 1985a, p. 37).

A number of feminist family therapists have written of the struggles and dilemmas of integrating feminist and family systems perspectives. Some suggest that such an integration is possible and that, by challenging it to include broader social contexts, feminist theory may enable family systems theory to become more truly systemic (Lerner, 1987; Taggart, 1985).

Goldner (1985b), however, sees feminism as dangerous to family therapy and believes that any "real encounter" between the two will involve a rethinking of many basic family therapy axioms and assumptions, as well as the introduction of new categories of analysis, such as gender, individual functioning, and "the material and social bases of interpersonal power . . . money, power, access to power, fairness, the ability to leave, and so on" (p. 23).

### Gender as a Fundamental Category

An emerging theme in the feminist critique of family therapy is an emphasis on gender as a major and "irreducible category of clinical observation and theorizing" (Goldner, 1985b, p. 22), similar in character to the basic categories of race and class. Reducing this elemental category to constructs such as "gender issues" and "gender roles" is seen as both trivializing gender and obscuring the reality of patriarchy as expressed in the power differences between genders (Goldner, 1985b; James, 1984; Thorne, 1985). The construct of sex roles implies that, similar to work or social roles, one can choose to "play" them or not, and that men and women are equally disadvantaged by this "common enemy" (Goldner, 1985b).

Several feminist writers argue strongly for the necessity of understanding the whole of human experience, including society, the family, and individual identity as being gendered, as well as for understanding the symbolic dimensions by which patriarchy is embedded in language, culture, and experience and thus subtly communicated and internalized from the moment of birth (Goldner, 1985b; James, 1984; Taggart, 1985).

### Tendency to Blame Mothers and Idealize Fathers

Feminists have expressed deep concern over subtle biases in family therapy theory which result in attributing responsibility to women for causing family problems as well as for changing them (Bograd, 1984; Layton, 1984). This concern may surprise many, since family therapy has prided itself on employing a nonblaming notion of systemic interaction which involves neither victims nor villains. However, by this very stance, family systems theory removes individual responsibility by simultaneously implying that men are not ultimately responsible for their actions and that women are coresponsible for violence enacted against them. Subtle assumptions of women's primary responsibility for childrearing underlie much of family therapy practice, resulting in a tendency to view children's problems as primarily caused by their mothers. Although emphasis is placed on involving fathers in family therapy, it is often with a view to helping mothers out, giving them a holiday, or teaching them more effective parenting skills.

Mother-blaming is prevalent in major clinical journals in several disciplines, and most strongly so in *Family Process* and psychoanalytic journals (Caplan & Hall-McCorquodale, 1984). These researchers found that two-thirds of the authors in nine major clinical journals, across three target years (1972, 1976, and 1982) attributed responsibility to mothers for a total of 72 different types of psychopathology in their children. They also documented a parallel tendency in clinical journals to idealize fathers, to describe them in only positive terms, and to not see their behavior (or nonbehavior) as contributing to their children's difficulties. Perhaps most disappointing of all was the finding that mother-blaming had not decreased in frequency over the 10-year period studied.

### Reinforcing Traditional Roles and Values

A recurrent theme regarding family therapy practice relates to what Hare-Mustin (1978) calls the "unquestioned reinforcement of stereotyped sex roles [that] takes place in much of family therapy" (p. 181). Feminists argue that family therapists often have stereotypical expectations of men and women, accept traditional relationship arrangements as the ideal (or at least as the most functional) and do not adequately appreciate the impact of traditional socialization on women, as well as on the development of family dysfunction. As a result of these assumptions, feminists suggest that family therapists often respond differentially to men and women and behave in ways which reinforce stereotyped roles and behaviors, whether intentionally or not (Avis, 1985a; Gurman & Klein, 1984; Hare-Mustin, 1978, 1979, 1980; Jacobson, 1983; Margolin, Fernandez, Talovic & Onorato, 1983).

These traditional expectations and assumptions derive in part from the male-based, male-focused theories of development, behavior and relationships which have been central to American professional education during the past 40 years. Weiner and Boss (1985) point out that as a result of these androcentric theories, most therapists view their clients through the distorted lens of male-defined reality and through theories which frequently blame women and view their socialized behaviors as signs of inherent weakness, passivity, or masochism.

The American Psychological Association Task Force on Sex Bias and Sex Role Stereotyping in Psychotherapeutic Practice (1975) identified four major sources of sex bias or sex role stereotyping as prevalent in clinical practice in general: (1) fostering traditional sex roles; (2) bias in expectations for women and devaluation of women; (3) sexist use of psychoanalytic concepts; and (4) responding to women as sex objects.

In addition, they found the following four biases particularly prevalent among family therapists: (1) assuming that remaining in a marriage would result in better adjustment for women; (2) demonstrating less interest and sensitivity to a woman's career than a man's; (3) perpetuating the belief that a child's problems and child-rearing are primarily women's responsibility; (4) exhibiting a double standard regarding wife's versus husband's extramarital affair; and (5) deferring to the husband's needs over the wife's. Although these findings are now more than 10 years old, the continued existence of these and other gender biases among family therapists is indicated both by Caplan and Hall-McCorquodale's (1984) finding of the current prevalence of mother-blaming in a major family therapy journal, and by recent feminist writings in the field (Avis, 1985a; Bograd, 1984; Jacobson, 1983; James, 1984; James & McIntyre, 1983; Margolin et al., 1983; Weiner & Boss, 1985).

### Ignoring the Political Dimensions of Family Therapy

Another feminist concern relates to the tendency of family therapists to ignore or deny the political aspects of what they do. Many therapists attempt to take a neutral stance regarding gender arrangements in the families they work with, believing that such a stance shows maximum respect for a family's values. What has been pointed out by feminist writers is that power is inherent in the therapeutic relationship, that therapists cannot *not* express values, and that therapeutic neutrality is an impossible and dangerous myth (Jacobson, 1983). Therapists who adhere to this myth inadvertently adopt political positions without knowing it, and, by what they choose to focus on, respond to, challenge, or ignore, they may inadvertently reinforce traditional values oppressive to women. Such reinforcement occurs primarily by default, i.e., the therapist's failure to challenge traditional arrangements is frequently perceived by clients as tacit approval (Jacobson, 1983). It is thus essential for therapists to be aware of their own values and beliefs and to be conscious of what values they are, indeed, reinforcing (Avis, 1985a, 1985b; Gurman & Klein, 1984; Jacobson, 1983; Weiner & Boss, 1985).

In recognition of this need for awareness, the Canadian Psychological Association adopted Guidelines for Therapy and Counselling with Women in 1980. The preamble to these guidelines states that therapists should:

> be aware of the impact their own socialization has had on them and recognize the potential biases against which they must guard. Those offering psychotherapy or counselling to women have an obligation to be knowledgeable about the current literature concerning sex bias and sex role stereotyping, to continually reassess their own values and attitudes in the light of new evidence, and to be especially sensitive to the fact that women may be especially disadvantaged by the power relationships between therapist/counsellor and client. (Canadian Psychological Association, 1980)

No similar guidelines have as yet been developed or adopted by the American Association for Marriage and Family Therapy.

### Gender Issues in Family Therapy Training

Feminists emphasize the central importance of gender and sex-role issues in both the content and process of family therapy training (Avis, 1986; Caust, Libow & Raskin, 1981; Okun, 1983; Wheeler, Avis, Miller & Chaney, 1985). Major issues involve the failure to include in family therapy training programs content related to gender and power or current research and theory regarding women; the teaching of theories and interventions which disadvantage women;

difficulties in training both men and women in behaviors which are contrary to their socialization (i.e., directive, task-oriented skills for women and affective, expressive skills for men); and gender issues which arise in the training process itself, in interactions between supervisor and trainee, between trainees, or between trainee and family. Concern regarding family therapy's inattention to gender in both the content and process of training is substantiated by the failure of the American Association for Family Therapy Commission on Accreditation (AAMFT, 1981) to require course content on gender or women. It is also borne out by a study of graduate-level curriculum for marriage and family therapy education (Winkle, Piercy & Hovestadt, 1981). Winkle et al.'s (1980) national panel of 25 training directors of graduate-level marriage and family therapy programs and 20 AAMFT Approved Supervisors mention gender in only one of 63 clinically related course content areas they consider important. Further, 47 of the 63 areas are rated as more important than that of gender.

Feminist recommendations regarding training include required readings and course content dealing with feminist theory and gender issues, analysis of videotapes to identify sex role and power behaviors by both therapist and family members, use of group supervision to explore trainees' feelings and values concerning gender roles and issues, Bowenian family of origin work focusing on the therapist's own sex-role issues, and providing training experiences, such as assertiveness training and behavior rehearsal, which help trainees develop nonstereotypical behaviors.

### Feminist Alternatives

Beginning with Hare-Mustin's (1978) suggestions for a feminist approach to family therapy, feminists in the field have written about their attempts to integrate feminist theory and values into their clinical work. Some have suggested specific techniques and interventions, while others, such as Goldner (1985a, 1985b) have simply raised provocative questions and cautioned against facile or simplistic solutions to complex and fundamental issues. Recent attempts at integration have moved beyond the tentative suggestion stage and feminist family therapists are writing of their clinical dilemmas and thinking processes and of their varying degrees of success in applying feminist principles to their practice. Specific alternatives include *talking* about gender issues during therapy (money, power, childcare, housework, the division of labor, etc); being direct about the therapist's own beliefs; relabeling deviance and redefining normality so as to highlight women's strengths; using Bowen family systems theory to aid women in defining themselves independently of what others expect them to be; focusing on the needs of women as individuals as well as on the needs of the relationship; avoiding conjoint therapy in cases of wife abuse; and empowering women in a wide variety of ways both inside and outside the therapy room (Avis, 1985a; Bepko, 1985; Bograd, 1984; Goldner, 1985a, 1985b; Goodrich, Rampage, Ellman & Halstead, 1985; Hare-Mustin, 1978, 1980; Jacobson, 1983; Lerner, 1985; Margolin et al., 1983, Weiner & Boss, 1985; Wheeler, 1985; Wheeler, Avis, Miller & Chaney, 1985).

The annotated bibliography at the end of this article suggests many readings which offer a deeper examination and understanding of gender issues in family therapy.

## FEMINIST THEORY AND FRAMEWORKS

Feminism is not monolithic. There are, rather, several different "feminisms," each based on a different conceptual analysis of women's subordination and each drawing on different theoretical traditions. While certain basic assumptions and goals are shared, feminists often differ strongly over specific issues as a result of conceptual differences which lead them to different interpretations, solutions and foci for change. A feminist framework is defined by Jaggar and Rothenberg (1984, p. xii) as a "comprehensive analysis of the nature and causes of women's oppression and a correlated set of proposals for ending it."

Jaggar and Rothenberg (1984) distinguish three major feminist frameworks which will be briefly summarized below. Appreciating how each conceptualizes women's oppression is helpful in understanding the theoretical basis of differing approaches and solutions proposed by feminist scholars in family therapy.

### Liberal Feminism

Growing out of the liberalism of 17th and 18th century political theorists and philosophers, liberal feminism emphasizes equality in terms of equal rights and equal opportunity for women. The liberal tradition viewed freedom as meaning freedom from interference, especially from government. Such freedom was seen as enabling individuals to advance according to their own talents and abilities, unhampered by external regulations or barriers. To the liberal, then, equality meant equality of opportunity.

Liberal feminists believe women's oppression results from legal constraints and social policies which discriminate against women and result in unequal civil rights and unequal educational and occupational opportunities. Liberal feminism does not attempt a historical analysis of the causes of this discrimination, but rather focuses effort on removing economic and legal barriers to women's equality. For the liberal feminist, the key to women's liberation lies in the removal of sexist discrimination (Jaggar & Rothenberg, 1984). The policies and efforts of the National Organization for Women are a good example of this framework. Betty Friedan, whose *Feminine Mystique* is often credited with beginning the current wave of the women's movement in the late 1960s, is a contemporary liberal feminist. Friedan (1963) believed that it was women's prescribed roles within the home and lack of opportunities without that resulted in a general malaise ("feminine mystique") in middle-class housewives of the 1960s. Her solution was to free women by giving them equal access to education and employment opportunities. Liberal feminists tend to distinguish between the personal and public lives of women, and focus their attention on removing barriers to women's equal participation in the public sphere (for example, elimination of sex discrimination in employment, provision of child care centers, equal education, and job training).

## Socialist Feminism

As its name implies, socialist feminism draws on Marxist traditions in its analysis of women's oppression. Like traditional Marxists, socialist feminists believe that human nature is not biologically determined, but is created by the type of society and form of social organization in which people live. They also agree with Marxists that it is impossible for people to have equal opportunity while living in a class society. However, unlike traditional Marxists, they do not view women's oppression as simply a result of the more pervasive and fundamental class oppression — i.e., as a result of capitalism rather than of sexism. Socialist feminists argue that although Marxist analysis is useful for "understanding conflicts between classes of men . . . it obscures certain features of women's oppression that cut across class lines" (Jaggar & Rothenberg, 1984, p. 77-78). They suggest that, in order to understand the oppression of women across classes, Marxist theory must be expanded from an analysis of the means of production to include an analysis of how the means of *reproduction* (including sexuality, nurturing, and raising children) are organized and distributed in society.

Such an expansion is necessary in order to analyze why women in every class are subordinate to men, both within the family and without. As Hartmann (1984, p. 174) points out, "the categories of Marxist analysis, class, reserve army of labor, wage-laborer, do not explain why particular people fill particular places" and why men dominate women in every sphere. Hartmann (1984) argues that patriarchy and capitalism are reciprocal and mutually reinforcing systems which allow men to control women's labor, and which must both be abolished if women are to be liberated.

## Radical Feminism

Unlike liberal and socialist feminisms which draw on traditional theoretical systems, radical feminism is a relatively new and evolving framework (Jaggar & Rothenberg, 1984). Radical feminism takes a number of different forms, arising from varying belief systems. However, all are based on the assumption that the oppression of women is the fundamental oppression — i.e., that it has operated across time, across culture, across class — and that it is embedded in every aspect of life, including language, and is therefore the hardest form of oppression to eradicate. Radical feminism emphasizes that the personal is political — i.e., that what happens in the private sphere, in women's personal lives, is an expression of their oppression in the wider public sphere. The personal is not just personal — it is the arena where women's subordinate position is enacted and reproduced. Radical feminists focus on the psychological and argue that "women's discontent . . . is not the neurotic lament of the maladjusted, but a response to a social structure in which women are systematically dominated, exploited, and oppressed" (Hartmann, 1984, p. 175). That social structure, according to radical feminists, is patriarchy, the system through which men of different races, classes, and cultures join together in their domination over women (Hartmann, 1984).

This framework finds expression in family therapy in the work of such feminist writers as Goldner (1985a, 1985b), James (1984), and James and McIntyre (1983), who emphasize gender as a fundamental category of human existence, power (and gender-linked power differences) as a basic dimension in marital and family relationships, and patriarchy as an interlocking system of meanings and symbols which organize our world.

## Feminism and Women of Color

The writings of women of color emphasize the intricate relationship between sex, race, and class; the importance of studying the complexities of these three categories together; and the error of assuming that women of different races and cultures experience sexual oppression in the same way (Jaggar & Rothenberg, 1984). Minority women suffer the double jeopardy of being both nonwhite and female, and their experience of discrimination is very different from that of their relatively privileged middle-class white sisters. Minority feminists often accuse the contemporary feminist movement of involving itself primarily with the concerns of white middle-class women, and ignoring those of women of color. As a result, many minority women feel greater solidarity with men of their own race than with white women (Hood, 1984).

## THE FEMINIST CRITIQUE OF THE FAMILY

The institution of the family, as traditionally structured and presently idealized, has come under wide-ranging criticism from feminist scholars in many fields. Bernard (1982) points out the "his" and "hers" dimensions of marriage and argues that women, men, girls, and boys do not experience marriage or their families in the same way. Feminists challenge a number of basic assumptions about families, including the ideology of the "monolithic family" which posits the traditional nuclear family as the only legitimate family form (Collier, Rosaldo & Yanagisako, 1982; Eichler, 1983; Tilly & Scott, 1978); the glorification of motherhood, and notions of the family as a haven, which are in disjunction with the realities of violence, conflict, and subordination which characterize many women's lives (Bernard, 1975; Chodorow & Contratto, 1982; Rich, 1976; Ruddick, 1982); assumptions of the normality, naturalness and inevitability of male dominance, of motherhood, of the sexual division of labor, and of heterosexuality (Rich, 1980; Hartmann, 1976); and assumptions of a commonality in family members' interests, or that an individual's needs are best met through the family (Eichler, 1981, 1983; Thorne, 1982). Feminists view women's subordination and economic exploitation as maintained by traditional family ideology, roles, and arrangements. In particular, they point to women's unpaid labor in the family, their economic dependence, isolation, and exclusion from direct sources of status, power, and material resources, as directly related to their segregation in low-paying job ghettos and exploitation in the marketplace (Hartmann, 1976; Oakley, 1974). Men's power and women's lack of it are regarded as major causes of women's social, emotional, psychological, and economic problems.

Feminists also challenge prevalent family theories, such as structural functionalism and role theory, which suggest that any one specific family form or arrangement is immutable, inevitable, and ultimately most functional (Thorne, 1982).

In addition to challenging the family as an institution, feminists also question the way in which the family is traditionally studied. They suggest that family research is permeated with androcentric biases which make invisible the differences in men's and women's experiences in the family; which ask different questions of men and women based on sexist assumptions (for example, whether mothers', but not fathers', employment outside the home has a negative effect on children); which fail to recognize the range of contemporary family forms as normal and legitimate in their own right (rather than as deviant in comparison with the traditional norm); and which fail to study the family in terms of its location within the ideological, political, and economic systems which mold it (Eichler, 1983; Thorne, 1982).

## RESEARCH ON SEX DIFFERENCES

There now exists a massive body of literature, developed in various disciplines over the past decades, concerning the differences and similarities between women and men on many dimensions. As biologists, psychologists, psychoanalysts, sex researchers, economists, behaviorists, sociologists, historians, and anthropologists each study sex differences from their own professional and personal perspectives, there has emerged a great deal of debate over how best to explain and interpret these differences (Caplan, MacPherson & Tobin, 1985; Tavris & Wade, 1984). Some suggest they are biological in origin (caused by differences in genes, hormones or brain structure and organization), others suggest they are caused by differences in personality resulting from anatomical differences, while still others suggest that differences in socialization, learning, and experience offer the best explanation. Another perspective looks to economic and political conditions as a major determinant of the social ideology, cultural values, and customs which in turn determine "appropriate" sex roles and behaviors (Tavris & Wade, 1984).

The research in psychology and sociology is of particular relevance for family therapists. Some areas of greatest interest are studies on the processes and sources of sex typing and sex role socialization (Baumrind, 1980; Bem, 1974, 1981); male and female differences in nonverbal communication (Fishman, 1978; Henley, 1977; Thorne & Henley, 1975); the feminization of poverty (Cocks, 1982; Tavris & Wade, 1984); sex differences in employment, status, power, and income (Crosby, 1982; Epstein, 1976; Treiman & Hartmann, 1981); sex differences in marital experience and satisfaction (Bernard, 1982; Ferree, 1976); time studies on the division of domestic labor and child care (Vanek, 1974; Strasser, 1982); studies of the relationship between mental health and marital status (Gove, 1972; Gove & Tudor, 1973; Weissman & Klerman, 1977); and studies of marital violence (Straus, Gelles, & Steinmetz, 1980; Yllo, 1983). The easiest and quickest way to gain an overview of major findings and themes is to read a review article or book which summarizes the findings of many studies, such as Deaux (1984) or Tavris and Wade (1984).

## RESEARCH ON WOMEN AND MENTAL HEALTH

The research and literature concerning women and mental health is of vital importance to family therapists. Phyllis Chesler, in *Women and Madness* (1972), first brought the abuses of women by the mental health system to public attention. Since then the relationship between sex, marital status and mental health, as well as the sexist treatment of women by mental health professionals have been extensively researched (Penfold & Walker, 1983). Study after study has found that women suffer from significantly higher rates of mental illness, especially depression, than men (Gove, 1972; Gove & Tudor, 1973; Radloff, 1975; Weissman, 1980; Weissman & Klerman, 1977). Gove and Tudor (1973) report that women have poorer self-images than men and report personal discomfort and psychiatric symptoms twice as frequently. In a major national survey, Veroff et al., (1981) found that "women are more demoralized than men . . . women, more than men, report difficulties in their daily lives . . . women find life more problematic than men" (p. 373). They conclude that these results indicate that "women's life situations confront them with experiences which put them in a more vulnerable position than men, a position that engenders psychological difficulties" (Veroff et al., 1981, p. 374).

Research has implicated a number of sociocultural factors in the greater stress and poorer mental health experienced by women. Among these are social factors such as traditional marital roles (Weissman & Klerman, 1977); economic factors such as low paying, high stress, dead-end "pink" ghetto jobs (Carmen et al., 1981); poor child support and the "feminization" of poverty; psychological factors such as learned helplessness and feelings of inadequacy and guilt (Miller, 1985); and political and legal factors such as an inability to exert influence or control over one's environment or life conditions; inadequate protection against abuse; discrimination in employment; lack of paid maternity leave; and lack of good quality, affordable child care.

In addition to women suffering from recognized forms of mental illness, others need specialized mental health services as a result of their particular vulnerability to sociocultural stresses. These include battered women, rape victims, poor women, minority women, women having abortions, and those living in rural environments (Mowbray, Lanir & Hulce, 1985). Because of women's more problematic life situations and greater vulnerability to psychological difficulties, most women need *appropriate* help at particular times or stages in their lives (Miller, 1985). Research on the sexist treatment of women in mental health settings, on clinicians' sex biases, and on the sexual exploitation of women clients, led to recognition of the need for alternative, innovative, and nonoppressive ways of helping women (Chesler, 1972; Greenspan, 1983; Penfold & Walker, 1983). Feminist therapy and counseling has developed during the past decade as such an alternative. This approach is based on a positive view of women as competent and as the best experts on themselves, on an understanding of women's problems as socially and culturally induced, and on a commitment to the full development of women.

Feminist therapists employ specific strategies for enhancing and validating women. These include deliberate efforts to reduce the hierarchy between therapist and client; an emphasis and focus on strength; an avoidance of diagnostic tests and labels; the use of therapeutic contracts in order to give women more control over their own therapy; the use of social analysis to help women understand the impact of social and cultural factors on their lives and their problems; sex role analysis to increase awareness of the processes of gender socialization and the costs of stereotypical roles; teaching skill building, stress management, and assertiveness training; and working with women in groups in order to provide support and contact, break down isolation, and increase awareness of the commonality of women's problems and their relation to societal roles and constraints (Collier, 1982; Gilbert, 1980; Greenspan, 1983; Israel, 1985; Rawlings & Carter, 1977; Russell, 1984; Sturdivant, 1980; Wheeler, 1985).

## CONTEMPORARY THEORY AND RESEARCH ON WOMEN'S DEVELOPMENT

In the recent past, a call for what Weiner and Boss (1985) refer to as "conceptual affirmative action—a rethinking of gender-role issues based on research and theory development about women over the life cycle" (p. 15) has been increasingly heard from feminist scholars in other fields. This literature provides positive alternatives for valuing women's capacities and for understanding women in their own right, rather than as "other" to man's norm.

Perhaps most notable of these new theoretical perspectives has been the work on mothering, particularly that of Chodorow (1978) and Dinnerstein (1976). Chodorow's theory of the social construction of the psychological processes of mothering has been repeatedly drawn on by feminist family therapists as helpful for expanding understanding of the relationship between family functioning and the socioeconomic context, as well as for understanding the development and maintenance ("reproduction") of different roles and relational capacities in men and women (Goldner 1985a, 1985b; James, 1984; James & McIntyre, 1983; Layton, 1984; Luepnitz, 1982; Okun, 1983; Weiner & Boss, 1985). Chodorow links the sexual division of labor to the economic requirements of Western capitalism, which result in women working primarily in the home and men primarily outside. She argues that the resulting allocation to women of primary responsibility for child care results in psychological processes through which girls identify with their mothers, develop female relational capacities, and grow up to be mothers themselves, while boys identify themselves as different from their mothers, separate psychologically from them, and grow up to be absent fathers involved in the world outside the home. Chodorow concludes that this division of labor, roles, and relationship capacities will continue to be reproduced in families as long as women continue to be the primary caretakers of children.

Dinnerstein's (1976) work is also cited extensively by feminist family therapists as helpful in understanding the relation between conventional parenting arrangements and the distinctly different ways in which male and female power is experienced (Goldner, 1985a; Layton, 1984; Luepnitz, 1982; Weiner & Boss, 1985). Dinnerstein (1976) hypothesizes that the domination of infant care by women results in exaggerated images and deep-seated fears of women's power, in views of women's power as irrational and engulfing, and in a tendency to displace rage at adult powerlessness onto women. Fathers' peripheral involvement in the early phases of their children's lives, on the other hand, results in men's power being experienced as much more restrained and objective, much less fearful and engulfing. Dinnerstein argues that female-dominated child care has profound implications for the development of misogyny in all its forms, including environmental destruction.

A number of other feminist theorists have provided conceptual frameworks which challenge traditional assumptions regarding women's behavior and psychosocial development. Prominent among these is Jean Baker Miller (1976) whose *Toward a New Psychology of Women* provides a model of adulthood based not on the male model of separation, but on a female-influenced model of connectedness, i.e., of valuing, enlarging, and deepening human relationships. Miller's model validates women's traditional capacities for nurturing and relationship, and suggests that as capacities essential to the human community they must be valued and shared by men as well as by women.

In another area of study, Caplan (1985) has examined and systematically debunked the myth of women's masochism. This destructive concept has permeated the mental health field since Freud first articulated it, and has been consistently used to explain why women stay in abusive marriages or unhappy relationships, or sacrifice themselves for their children. Caplan analyzes women's traditional behavior in terms of its social context and finds that what has often been mislabeled as masochistic is actually the ability to "wait for rewards, . . . put other people's needs ahead of one's own; . . . the belief . . . that what one has is about all one can expect to get; or the effort to *avoid* punishment, rejection, or guilt" (p. 14).

Carol Gilligan's (1982) research on women's moral development is highly significant and enlightening. When she discovered that Kohlberg's esteemed model of moral development had been developed from research done only on males, she set out to replicate his research with females. Her work not only distinguishes women's moral development as different from men's (women emphasize relationships, social context, caring, and responsibility, while men emphasize rights, logic, and hierarchy); it also demonstrates the vulnerability of social science to invisible bias, the tendency to judge women by male norms, and the fallacy of assuming that theory and research developed on men applies equally to women.

Some of the most important readings in this area are the works of the feminist theorists discussed above. They are listed in the annotated readings.

## CONCLUSION

This paper has delineated some of the major recurring themes in the feminist critique of family therapy, as well as relevant feminist theory and research from other disciplines. It is hoped that this overview is sufficient to allow clinicians to gain a sense of the major issues and questions central to feminist concerns, as well as of the scholarly foundation upon which they are based. It is also hoped that this overview, along with the annotated suggested readings which follow, will enable the reader to develop a personalized study plan based on the questions of greatest interest to her or him. Most of the readings contain their own suggestions for further study — once begun, such an exploration tends to develop a life of its own.

## ANNOTATED BIBLIOGRAPHY
## AND RECOMMENDATIONS FOR FURTHER READING

### The Feminist Critique of Family Therapy

Ault-Riché, M. (Ed.). (1986). *Women and family therapy*. Rockville, MD: Aspen systems.
  This edited volume is the first that focuses specifically on issues related to women and family therapy. Its ten chapters,

written by many well-known feminist family therapists, cover a wide range of therapeutic topics and provide an overview of some areas of concern to feminists in the field.

Avis, J.M. (1985). The politics of functional family therapy: A feminist critique. *Journal of Marital and Family Therapy, 11*, 127-138.
This article examines the political processes and gender biases inherent in functional family therapy. It argues that this model subtly reinforces traditional gender roles in both family and therapist, and examines the implications of this bias.

Bograd, M. (1984). Family systems approaches to wife battering: A feminist critique. *American Journal of Orthopsychiatry, 54*, 558-563.
This incisive analysis demonstrates how subtle biases implicit in systems formulations are translated into practice, rendering it an inadequate conceptual framework in situations of violence and abuse.

Caplan, P. J. & Hall-McCorquodale, I. (1985). Mother-blaming in major clinical journals. *American Journal of Orthopsychiatry, 55*, 345-353.
This fascinating study reports vivid examples of mother-blaming and father-idealizing in clinical journals. A great consciousness raiser regarding subtle biases in the literature.

Carter, E., Papp, P., Silverstein, O. & Walters, M. (1983). *Mothers and daughters*. Monograph Series, 1(1). Washington: The Women's Project in Family Therapy.

Carter, E., Papp, P., Silverstein, O. & Walters, M. (1984). *Mothers and sons, fathers and daughters*. Monograph Series, 2(1). Washington: The Women's Project in Family Therapy.
These monographs are collections of authors' conference presentations which reflect on the politics of gender in parent-child relationships. The paradoxical injunctions inherent in mothers' relationships with both daughters and sons are particularly well explored, as are the implications for family therapists of traditional formulations and interventions.

Caust, B. L., Libow, J. A. & Raskin, P. A. (1981). Challenges and promises of training women as family systems therapists. *Family Process, 20*, 439-447.

A discussion of challenges related to gender socialization and sexual politics which may arise in training women as family therapists, and of the role of a feminist orientation in empowering trainees and promoting nonstereotypical behavior.

Goldner, V. (1985a). Feminism and family therapy. *Family Process, 24,* 31-47.
An eloquent and scholarly feminist analysis of family therapy ideology and of the complexities and dilemmas of sexual politics in family therapy practice. If you have time to read only one article, this is it.

Goldner, V. (1985b). Warning: Family therapy may be dangerous to your health. *The Family Therapy Networker, 9,* 19-23.
A thought-provoking paper which proposes the universality of gender as a basic category of human organization and domination, and the necessity to rethink core family therapy assumptions in order to account for gender and power differences. Important reading.

Gurman, A. S. & Klein, M. H. (1984). Marriage and the family: An unconscious male bias in behavioral treatment? In E. A. Blechman (Ed.), *Behavior modification with women.* New York: Guilford Press.
This chapter critiques the unconscious gender bias inherent in the philosophy and practice of behavioral marital and family therapy. The authors argue persuasively that the clarification and acknowledgment of the therapist's own personal and professional values are essential to avoid this bias in practice.

Hare-Mustin, R. T. (1978). A feminist approach to family therapy. *Family Process, 17,* 181-194.
This pioneering article was the first to raise feminist concerns in family therapy. It examines the unquestioned reinforcement of traditional gender roles in practice and offers many suggestions for applying a feminist consciousness to family therapy. Important reading.

Jacobson, N. (1983). Beyond empiricism: The politics of marital therapy. *American Journal of Family Therapy, 11,* 11-24.
This article provides an excellent discussion of the political issues inherent in therapy in general and behavioral marital therapy (BMT) in particular. Jacobson identifies the processes through which traditional values and roles oppressive to

women are inadvertently reinforced in BMT and makes specific recommendations for changing them.

James, K. (1984). Breaking the chains of gender. *Australian Journal of Family Therapy, 5*, 241-248.
A thought-provoking discussion of the symbolic dimensions of patriarchy which embed male dominance and female subordination in all aspects of culture. An excellent article.

James, K. & McIntyre, D. (1983). The reproduction of families: The social role of family therapy? *Journal of Marital and Family Therapy, 9*, 119-129.
The authors challenge family therapy's failure to respond to recent critical analyses of the family, or to consider the socioeconomic and political contexts of family functioning. They also examine the limitations and consequences of systems theory as employed in this field. This scholarly analysis is highly recommended.

Layton, M. (1984). Tipping the therapeutic balance: Masculine, feminine or neuter? *The Family Therapy Networker, 8*, 21-27.
This short, well-written article touches on many gender issues that arise in family therapy, particularly the tendency to blame mothers and hold them responsible for family change. The author includes her own very helpful annotated guide to the literature.

Libow, J. A., Raskin, P. A. & Caust, B. L. (1982). Feminist and family systems therapy: Are they irreconcilable? *The American Journal of Family Therapy, 10*, 3-12.
This article identifies the differences and commonalities between feminist and family therapies in both theory and technique. Helpful for understanding and comparing the two frameworks.

Margolin, G., Fernandez, R., Talovic, S. & Onorato, R. (1983). Sex role considerations and behavioral marital therapy: Equal does not mean identical. *Journal of Marital and Family Therapy, 9*, 131-145.
The authors identify a variety of ways in which behavioral marital therapy (BMT) gives contradictory messages regarding sex role issues. They make recommendations for how BMT can become more sensitive to these issues as well as more flexible in handling them.

Okun, B. F. (1983). Gender issues of family systems therapists. In B. A. Okun & S. T. Gladding (Eds.), *Issues in training marriage and family therapists*. Ann Arbor, MI: ERIC/CAPS.
This chapter provides a good introduction to gender issues in both the training of family therapists and the practice of family therapy.

Simon, R. (Ed.) (1985). Feminism: Shedding new light on the family. *Family Therapy Networker* (Special Issue), *9*(6).
This special issue of the *Family Therapy Networker* takes a serious look at the impact of feminism on family therapy and the application of feminist principles to practice. Thought provoking articles and case studies make this important reading.

Taggart, M. (1985). The feminist critique in epistemological perspective: Questions of context in family therapy. *Journal of Marital and Family Therapy, 11*, 113-126.
A thoughtful and comprehensive discussion of the feminist critique of systemic epistemology, in which the author suggests that this critique may challenge systems theory to become more truly systemic by including broader contexts.

Weiner, J. P. & Boss, P. (1985). Exploring gender bias against women: Ethics for marriage and family therapy. *Counseling and Values, 30*, 9-23.
These authors cast gender issues in family therapy in ethical terms and call for affirmative action in both theory and training. Most valuable are their ethical guidelines for reducing gender bias in family therapy.

Wheeler, D., Avis, J. M., Miller, L. & Chaney, S. (1985). Rethinking family therapy education and supervision: A feminist model. *Journal of Psychotherapy & the Family, 1*, 53-71.
These authors suggest a framework for a feminist approach to family therapy training. They delineate feminist perceptual, conceptual and executive skills, as well as methods for teaching them.

The Women's Project in Family Therapy (in press). *Women in families: Implications for family therapy*. New York: Guilford.
An analysis of women in various relationships in the family, with case studies that illustrate a feminist approach to working with those relationships. Of particular interest is the fact that although the case studies share a feminist perspective, they represent differing theoretical orientations to family therapy.

## Feminist Theory and Frameworks

Eisenstein, H. (1983). *Contemporary feminist thought*. Boston: G. K. Hall.
An excellent introduction and guide to contemporary feminist thought in America. Written for readers unfamiliar with feminism, it traces the evolution of feminist thought since 1970 and helps make sense of changing ideas. Highly recommended.

Eisenstein, Z. (1984). *Feminism and sexual equality: Crisis in liberal America*. New York: Monthly Review Press.
An analysis of the growing conservatism in America and its impact on attitudes and policies concerning women. Articulate and provocative.

Jaggar, A. M. & Rothenberg, P. S. (Eds.) (1984). *Feminist frameworks: Alternative theoretical accounts of the relations between women and men* (2nd Ed.). New York: McGraw-Hill.
This edited volume offers an extremely helpful organization of major feminist theories. Excellent selections of lively and instructive readings. Highly recommended.

## The Feminist Critique of the Family

Ehrenreich, B. (1983). *The hearts of men: American dreams and the flight from commitment*. New York: Anchor Books.
An original and fascinating analysis of the changing bonds between men and women over the past 30 years.

Eichler, M. (1983). *Families in Canada today*. Toronto: Gage Publishing.
Particularly valuable for its delineation of four major biases in the family literature and for the challenging questions it raises regarding family literature and research. Although specifically focused on Canadian families, the issues apply equally to the U.S.

Mainardi, P. (1970). The politics of housework. In R. Morgan (Ed.) *Sisterhood is powerful*. New York: Vintage.
A delightfully funny early piece, painful in its accuracy.

Rich, A. (1976). *Of woman born: Motherhood as experience and institution*. New York: W.W. Norton.
Rich draws on her own experience as well as on research and literature to explore the "power and powerlessness embodied

in motherhood in patriarchal culture." Personal, intense, scholarly—a classic.

Rich, A. (1980). Compulsory heterosexuality and lesbian existence. *Signs: Journal of Women in Culture and Society, 5,* 631-660.
A challenge to the assumption that heterosexuality is "natural" through an examination of social and political pressures toward heterosexuality.

Rubin, L. (1983). *Intimate strangers: Men and women together.* New York: Harper & Row.
Rubin explores the sources of deeply engendered differences between men and women and the impact of these differences on intimacy, sexual relationships, love, work, identity, and parenting. With great sensitivity she examines the dilemmas, conflicts, and paradoxes which confront men and women as they negotiate new-age roles and rules with "old-age consciousness." This very fine book, essentially the clinical application of Chodorow's theories, is valuable for both therapists and clients.

Thorne, B. & Yalom, M. (Eds.) (1982). *Rethinking the family: Some feminist questions.* New York: Longman.
This outstanding edited volume presents feminist analysis and revisioning of the family from the perspectives of varied disciplines. The introductory chapter by Thorne is particularly helpful in its overview of themes and assumptions central to feminist critiques of the family. Highly recommended.

## Research on Sex Differences

Fishman, P. (1978). Interaction: The work women do. *Social Problems, 25,* 397-406.
A dramatic study of how gender hierarchy is established and maintained in everyday verbal interaction. The author analyzed tapes of daily conversations of male-female couples and found that women did most of the interactional work (asking questions, listening, responding) while men controlled the direction and content of the conversation. Illuminating.

Henley, N. (1977). *Body politics: Power, sex, and nonverbal communication.* Englewood Cliffs, NJ: Prentice-Hall.
A fascinating analysis of research on male-female differences in nonverbal communication, and on how these differences

express and maintain gender hierarchy. Important and entertaining reading.

Keller, E. F. (1985). *Reflections on gender and science*. New Haven: Yale University Press.
This is a highly readable, thought-provoking analysis of the relationship between gender and science. Keller writes from the perspective of a respected mathematician and starts from the assumption that both gender and science are socially constructed categories.

Tavris, D. & Wade, C. (Eds.) (1984). *The longest war: Sex differences in perspective*. New York: Harcourt, Brace, Jovanovich.
A presentation of the research on sex differences from the perspective of several different disciplines. Valuable not only for its summary of research findings, but for the light it sheds on the differing perspectives from which various disciplines approach the study of sex differences.

## Women and Mental Health

Brodsky, A. M. & Hare-Mustin, R. (Eds.) (1980). *Women and psychotherapy*. New York: Guilford Press.
A comprehensive examination of major issues concerning women and therapy, including research on gender differences in therapy, high-frequency disorders among women, critiques of traditional approaches, and alternative interventions. Excellent.

Broverman, I., Broverman, D., Clarkson, F., Rosenkrantz, P. & Vogel, S. (1970). Sex role stereotypes and clinical judgments of mental health. *Journal of Consulting and Clinical Psychology, 34*, 1-7.
This often-cited study examines clinicians' differential perceptions of and criteria for mental health in men and women. Findings reveal that while clinicians judged stereotypically masculine behavior as adult, they judged stereotypically feminine behavior as nonadult, leaving women with a choice of being regarded as adult but unfeminine, or as being feminine but nonadult.

Chesler, P. (1972). *Women and madness*. Garden City, NY: Doubleday.
A piercing analysis and indictment of how women have been

viewed and treated by psychiatric systems, as well as a call for a new psychology of women. A classic.

Ehrenreich, B. & English, D. (1978). *For her own good: 150 years of the experts' advice to women*. Garden City, NY: Anchor Books.
This fascinating book recounts a history of women's experience at the hands of professional "experts," especially doctors, from the witch hunts to the contemporary single woman. It is well-researched, witty, and highly illuminating. Must reading.

Greenspan, M. (1983). *A new approach to women and therapy*. New York: McGraw-Hill.
This wise, entertaining, and very human book presents the most thorough explication of individual feminist therapy yet available. The author uses clinical examples to critically examine traditional ways of thinking about and treating women, as well as to illustrate the theory and practice of feminist therapy. Highly recommended.

Lerner, H. G. (1985). *The dance of anger: A women's guide to changing the patterns of intimate relationships*. New York: Harper & Row.
The author brings together her systemic understanding of family relationships with her feminist understanding of women's experience to create a helpful guide for women in dealing with anger in important relationships. A valuable resource for both clients and therapists.

Mowbray, C. T., Lanir, S. & Hulce, M. (Eds.) (1985). *Women and mental health: New directions for change*. New York: Harrington Park Press.
A special issue of *Women & Therapy* which deals with the causes and treatment of women's mental health problems and innovative alternatives.

Penfold, P. S. & Walker, G. A. (1983). *Women and the psychiatric paradox*. Montreal: Eden Press.
The authors of this well researched and scholarly book present a thorough feminist critique of the institution of psychiatry, of its ideology and theory regarding women, and of its social control function in enforcing women's roles and controlling their activities. They also discuss feminist alternatives in theory and therapy. Highly recommended.

Russell, M. N. (1984). *Skills in counseling women: The feminist approach*. Springfield: Charles C Thomas.
Using a microskills teaching approach, the author outlines the step-by-step development of basic feminist counseling skills. Particularly useful as a teaching resource, the book also contains an excellent 40-page summary of the history and development of feminist counseling.

## Contemporary Theory and Research on Women's Development

Caplan, P. J. (1985). *The myth of women's masochism*. New York: E. P. Dutton.
A fascinating book which debunks the myth that women enjoy their oppression by examining women's stereotypical behavior in its social context. Excellent.

Chodorow, N. (1978). *The reproduction of mothering: Psychoanalysis and the sociology of gender*. Berkeley: University of California Press.
A ground-breaking analysis of the social and psychological consequences of women's mothering which provides a strong theoretical argument for the need for men and women to parent equally. Important.

Dinnerstein, D. (1976). *The mermaid and the minotaur: Sexual arrangements and human malaise*. New York: Harper & Row.
An eloquent and powerful analysis of the consequences of female-dominated child care for adult perceptions of women and female power.

Gilligan, C. (1982). *In a different voice: Psychological theory and women's development*. Cambridge: Harvard University Press.
This extremely important book is revolutionary in its impact. Gilligan's research on female moral development challenges Kohlberg's famous model which was developed on males, but claimed to be equally applicable to both sexes. A vivid illustration of invisible male bias in social science, as well as of the evaluation of women against male norms. Essential reading.

Miller, J. B. (1976). *Toward a new psychology of women*. Boston: Beacon Press.
A wonderful little book which redefines and validates women's experience and development. A good place to start.

# REFERENCES

American Association for Marriage and Family Therapy. *Manual on Accreditation*. Washington, DC: AAMFT, 1981.

American Association for Marriage and Family Therapy (1982). *Ethical principles for family therapists*. Washington, DC: AAMFT.

American Psychological Association Task Force (1975). Report of the task force on sex bias and sex-role stereotyping in psychotherapeutic practice. *American Psychologist, 30*, 1169-1175.

Avis, J. M. (1985a). The politics of functional family therapy: A feminist critique. *Journal of Marital and Family Therapy, 11*, 127-138.

Avis, J. M. (1985b). Through a different lens: A reply to Alexander, Warburton, Waldron, and Mas. *Journal of Marital and Family Therapy, 11*, 145-148.

Avis, J. M. (1986). Training and supervision in feminist-informed family therapy: A delphi study. Unpublished doctoral dissertation, Purdue University, West Lafayette, IN.

Baumrind, D. (1980). New directions in socialization research. *American Psychologist, 35*, 639-652.

Bem, S. L. (1974). The measurement of psychological androgyny. *Journal of Consulting and Clinical Psychology, 42*, 155-162.

Bem, S. L. (1981). Gender schema theory: A cognitive account of sex typing. *Psychological Review, 88*, 354-364.

Bepko, C. (1985). Mary and John: Power, power, who's got the power? *The Family Therapy Networker, 9*, 47-49.

Bernard, J. (1975). *The future of motherhood*. New York: Penguin Books.

Bernard, J. (1982). *The future of marriage* (2nd ed.). New Haven: Yale University Press.

Bograd, M. (1984). Family systems approaches to wife battering: A feminist critique. *American Journal of Orthopsychiatry, 54*, 558-568.

Brodsky, A. M. & Hare-Mustin, R. (Eds.) (1980). *Women and psychotherapy*. New York: Guilford Press.

Broverman, I., Broverman, D., Clarkson, F., Rosenkrantz, P. & Vogel, S. (1970). Sex role stereotypes and clinical judgments of mental health. *Journal of Consulting and Clinical Psychology, 34*, 1-7.

Canadian Psychological Association (1980). Guidelines for therapy and counselling with women. *Canadian Psychology, 21*.

Caplan, P. J. (1985). *The myth of women's masochism*. New York: E. P. Dutton.

Caplan, P. J. & Hall-McCorquodale, I. (1984). Mother-blaming in major clinical journals. *American Journal of Orthopsychiatry, 55*, 345-353.

Caplan, P. J., MacPherson, G. M. & Tobin, P. (1985). Do sex-related differences in spatial abilities exist? A multilevel critique with new data. *American Psychologist, 40*, 786-799.

Carmen, E., Russo, N. & Miller, J. (1981). Inequality and women's mental health: An overview. *American Journal of Psychiatry, 138*, 1319-1330.

Caust, B., Libow, J. & Raskin, P. (1981). Challenges and promises of training women as family systems therapists. *Family Process, 20*, 439-447. Chesler, P. (1972). *Women and madness*. New York: Doubleday.

Chesler, P. (1972). *Women and Madness*. Garden City, NY: Doubleday.

Chodorow, N. (1978). *The reproduction of mothering: Psychoanalysis and the sociology of gender*. Berkeley: University of California Press.

Chodorow, N. & Contratto, S. (1982). The fantasy of the perfect mother. In B. Thorne & M. Yalom (Eds.), *Rethinking the family: Some feminist questions*. New York: Longman.

Cocks, J. (1982). How long till equality? *Time*, July 12, 20-29.

Collier, H. V. (1982). *Counseling women: A guide for therapists*. New York: The Free Press.

Collier, J., Rosaldo, M. Z. & Yanagisako, S. (1982). Is there a family? New anthropological views. In B. Thorne & M. Yalom (Eds.), *Rethinking the family: Some feminist questions*. New York: Longman.

Crosby, F. (1982). *Relative deprivation and working women*. New York: Oxford.

Deaux, K. (1984). From individual differences to social categories. *American Psychologist, 39*, 105-116.

Dinnerstein, D. (1976). *The mermaid and the minotaur: Sexual arrangements and human malaise*. New York: Harper & Row.

Eichler, M. (1980). *The double standard: A feminist critique of feminist social science*. New York: St. Martin's Press.

Eichler, M. (1981). The inadequacy of the monolithic model of the family. *Canadian Journal of Sociology, 6*, 367-388.

Eichler, M. (1983). *Families in Canada today*. Toronto: Gage.

Eisenstein, H. (1983). *Contemporary feminist thought*. Boston: G. K. Hall.

Eisenstein, Z. (1984). *Feminism and sexual equality: Crisis in liberal America*. New York: Monthly Review Press.

Epstein, C. F. (1976). Separate and unequal. *Social Policy, 6*, 17-23.

Ferree, M. M. (1976). The confused American housewife. *Psychology Today, 10*, 76-80.

Fishman, P. (1978). Interaction: The work women do. *Social Problems, 25*, 397-406.

Friedan, B. (1963). *The feminine mystique*. New York: Dell Publishing.

Gilbert, L. A. (1980). Feminist therapy. In A. M. Brodsky & R. Hare-Mustin (Eds.), *Women and psychotherapy: An assessment of research and practice*. New York: Guilford Press.

Gilligan, C. (1982). *In a different voice: Psychological theory and women's development*. Cambridge: Harvard University Press.

Goldner, V. (1985a). Feminism and family therapy. *Family Process, 24*, 31-47.

Goldner, V. (1985b). Warning: Family therapy may be dangerous to your health. *The Family Therapy Networker, 9*, 19-23.

Goodrich, T. J., Rampage, C., Ellman, B. & Halstead, K. (1985). Angie and Hank. *The Family Therapy Networker, 9*, 50-52.

Gove, W. R. (1972). The relationship between sex roles, marital status, and mental illness. *Social Forces, 51*, 34-44.

Gove, W. R. & Tudor, J. (1973). Adult sex roles and mental illness. *American Journal of Sociology, 77*, 812-835.

Greenspan, M. (1983). *A new approach to women and therapy*. New York: McGraw-Hill.

Gurman, A. S. & Klein, M. H. (1984). Marriage and the family: An unconscious male bias in behavioral treatment? In E. A. Blechman (Ed.), *Behavior modification with women*. New York: Guilford Press.

Hare-Mustin, R. T. (1978). A feminist approach to family therapy. *Family Process, 17*, 181-194.

Hare-Mustin, R. T. (1979). Family therapy and sex role stereotypes. *The Counseling Psychologist, 8,* 31-32.

Hare-Mustin, R. T. (1980). Family therapy may be dangerous for your health. *Professional Psychology, 11,* 935-938.

Hartmann, H. (1976). Capitalism, patriarchy, and job segregation by sex. *Signs: Journal of Women in Culture and Society, 1,* 137-170.

Hartmann, H. (1984). The unhappy marriage of marxism and feminism: Towards a more progressive union. In A. M. Jaggar & P. S. Rothenberg (Eds.), *Feminist frameworks: Alternative theoretical accounts of the relations between women and men* (2nd ed.). New York: McGraw-Hill.

Henley, N. (1977). *Body politics: Power, sex, and nonverbal communication.* Englewood Cliffs, NJ: Prentice-Hall.

Hood, E. F. (1984). Black women, white women: Separate paths to liberation. In A. M. Jaggar & P. S. Rothenberg (Eds.), *Feminist frameworks: Alternative theoretical accounts of the relations between women and men* (2nd ed.). New York: McGraw-Hill.

Israel, J. (1985). Feminist therapy. In C. T. Mowbray, S. Lanir & M. Hulce (Eds.), *Women and Mental Health.* New York: Harrington Park Press.

Jacobson, N. S. (1983). Beyond empiricism: The politics of marital therapy. *American Journal of Family Therapy, 11,* 11-24.

Jaggar, A. M. & Rothenberg, P. S. (1984). *Feminist frameworks: Alternative theoretical accounts of the relations between women and men* (2nd ed.). New York: McGraw-Hill.

James, K. (1984). Breaking the chains of gender. *Australian Journal of Family Therapy, 5,* 241-248.

James, K. & McIntyre, D. (1983). The reproduction of families: The social role of family therapy? *Journal of Marital and Family Therapy, 9,* 119-129.

Keller, E. F. (1985). *Reflections on gender and science.* New Haven: Yale University Press.

Layton, M. (1984). Tipping the therapeutic balance: Masculine, feminine or neuter? *The Family Therapy Networker, 8,* 21-27.

Lerner, H. G. (1985). *The dance of anger: A women's guide to changing the patterns of intimate relationships.* New York: Harper & Row.

Lerner, H. G. (1987). Is family systems theory really systemic? A feminist communication. *Journal of Psychotherapy & the Family, 3.*

Libow, J. A., Raskin, P. A. & Caust, B. L. (1982). Feminist and family systems therapy: Are they irreconcilable? *The American Journal of Family Therapy, 10,* 3-12.

Luepnitz, D. (1982). *Child custody: A study of families after divorce.* Lexington, MA: Lexington Books.

Mainardi, P. (1970). The politics of housework. In R. Morgan (Ed.), *Sisterhood is powerful.* New York: Vintage.

Margolin, G., Fernandez, R., Talovic, S. & Onorato, R. (1983). Sex role considerations and behavioral marital therapy: Equal does not mean identical. *Journal of Marital and Family Therapy, 9,* 131-145.

Miller, J. B. (1976). *Toward a new psychology of women.* Boston: Beacon Press.

Miller, J. B. (1985). Women's mental health issues: Moving forward with awareness and program alternatives. In C. T. Mowbray, S. Lanir & M. Hulce (Eds.), *Women and Mental Health.* New York: Harrington Park Press.

Mowbray, C. T., Lanir, S., & Hulce, M. (Eds.) (1985). *Women and Mental Health*. New York: Harrington Park Press.

Oakley, A. (1974). *Woman's work: The housewife, past and present*. New York: Pantheon.

Okun, B. F. (1983). Gender issues of family systems therapists. In B. Okun & S. T. Gladding (Eds.), *Issues in training marriage and family therapists*. Ann Arbor, MI: ERIC/CAPS.

Penfold, P. S. & Walker, G. A. (1983). *Women and the psychiatric paradox*. Montreal: Eden Press.

Radloff, L. S. (1975). Sex differences in depression: The effects of occupation and marital status. *Sex Roles, 1*, 249-269.

Rawlings, E. I. & Carter, D. K. (1977). *Psychotherapy for women: Treatment toward equality*. Springfield: Charles C Thomas.

Rich, A. (1976). *Of woman born: Motherhood as experience and institution*. New York: W.W. Norton & Company, Inc.

Rich, A. (1980). Compulsory heterosexuality and lesbian existence. *Signs: Journal of Women in Culture and Society, 5*, 631-660.

Rubin, L. B. (1983). *Intimate strangers*. New York: Harper & Row.

Ruddick, S. (1982). Maternal thinking. In B. Thorne & M. Yalom, (Eds.), *Rethinking the family: Some feminist questions*. New York: Longman.

Simon, R. (Ed.) (1985). Feminism: Shedding new light on the family. *Family Therapy Networker* (Special Issue), *9*(6).

Strasser, S. (1982). *Never done: A history of American housework*. New York: Pantheon.

Straus, M., Gelles, R. & Steinmetz, S. (1980). *Behind closed doors: Violence in the American family*. Garden City, NY: Anchor/Doubleday.

Sturdivant, S. (1980). *Therapy with women: A feminist philosophy of treatment*. New York: Springer.

Taggart, M. (1985). The feminist critique in epistemological perspective: Questions of context in family therapy. *Journal of Marital and Family Therapy, 11*, 113-126.

Tavris, D. & Wade, C. (1984). *The longest war: Sex differences in perspective*. New York: Harcourt, Brace, Jovanovich.

Thorne, B. (1982). Feminist rethinking of the family: An overview. In B. Thorne & M. Yalom (Eds.), *Rethinking the family: Some feminist questions*. New York: Longman.

Thorne, B. (1985). Feminist rethinking of the family: Some feminist questions. Presentation to the Annual Conference of the National Council on Family Relations.

Thorne, B. & Henley, N. M. (Eds.) (1975). *Language and sex: Difference and dominance*. Rowley, MA: Newbury House.

Thorne, B. & Yalom, M. (Eds.) (1982). *Rethinking the family: Some feminist questions*. New York: Longman.

Tilly, L. & Scott, J. (1978). *Women, work, and family*. New York: Holt, Rinehart and Winston.

Treiman, D. & Hartmann, H. (Eds.) (1981). *Women, work, and wages*. Washington, DC: National Academy of Sciences Press.

Vanek, J. (1974). Time spent in housework. *Scientific American, 231*, 116-120.

Veroff, J., Douvan, E. & Kulka, R. A. (1981). *The inner American*. New York: Basic Books.

Weiner, J. P. & Boss, P. (1985). Exploring gender bias against women: Ethics for marriage and family therapy. *Counseling and Values, 30*, 9-23.

Weissman, M. M. (1980). Depression. In A. M. Brodsky & R. T. Hare-Mustin (Eds.), *Women and psychotherapy*. New York: Guilford Press.

Weissman, M. M. & Klerman, G. L. (1977). Sex differences and the epidemiology of depression. *Archives of General Psychiatry, 34*, 98-111.

Wheeler, D. (1985). The theory and practice of feminist-informed family therapy: A delphi study. Unpublished doctoral dissertation, Purdue University.

Wheeler, D., Avis, J., Miller, L. & Chaney, S. (1985). Rethinking family therapy training and supervision: A feminist model. *Journal of Psychotherapy & the Family, 1*, 53-71.

Winkle, W. C., Piercy, F. P. & Hovestadt, A. J. (1981). A curriculum for graduate-level marriage and family therapy education. *Journal of Marital and Family Therapy, 7*, 201-210.

Yllo, K. (1983). Sexual inequality and domestic violence in American states. *Journal of Comparative Family Studies*.

# THEORETICAL ISSUES

# Is Family Systems Theory
# Really Systemic?
# A Feminist Communication

### Harriet Goldhor Lerner

**SUMMARY.** Despite the fact that many systems theorists strive to pay primary attention to the rules and roles of an individual's context, the family literature tends to examine family dysfunction as if it unfolds in isolation from the broader patriarchal system in which the family is embedded. Viewed from this perspective, the author argues that Family Systems Theory is not contextual enough, and that much can be gained from beginning to seriously explore the circular interrelatedness of patriarchal society and the functioning of particular families.

Following many years of traditional training in individual psychotherapy, I am finding the contributions of family systems theory not only inspiring but something of a relief. The relief comes from discovering a sophisticated epistemological framework for the understanding of human problems that truly attempts not to blame mothers (or anyone else, for that matter), that roots theory and practice in the real world of specific interpersonal transactions as well as the factual history of a family's development, and that avoids the reification of "intrapsychic self" as separate and distinct from interpersonal context.

Harriet Goldhor Lerner, PhD, is Staff Psychologist, The Menninger Foundation, Topeka, KS.

From the start, however, I have been troubled by the question: "Is family systems theory *really* systemic?" My training at the Menninger Foundation first taught me that the system requiring attention and intervention is that of id, ego, and superego; later, the world of internalized objects and part-objects was added to the drama of impulse and defense. In contrast, the family literature redefines the system to include any and all family members who can come to the consulting room or fit on a genogram. But what of the larger system in which the family system is embedded? In researching the literature I have found that "culture" is about as important to systems thinkers as "family dynamics" is to psychoanalysts. It is given lip service, but for most family therapists it is not the "real stuff" of human interactions from which theory emerges and interventions are based.

Listening to Dr. Murray Bowen at a recent Georgetown Symposium, I imaged the multigenerational family system as being a connected group of little circles and squares suspended in space—hanging in a vacuum, as it were. Undoubtedly, Bowen theorists are aware that the family system is given its shape and form by the societal system, which reciprocally is shaped and formed by the family system. By definition, a systemic perspective views "family" and "society" as inextricably interwoven and circularly intertwined, inseparable one from the other. Yet Bowen and his colleagues (Bowen, 1978; Kerr, 1981), while attending to our interconnectedness with other biological life forms, have paid virtually no attention to the primary dysfunction of the patriarchal sociocultural system and the profound implications that this larger context has for dysfunctional patterns of family development and specific obstacles that block the differentiation of self.[1]

What of the majority of other family therapists working from different theoretical approaches? As recently as 1983, a commentor on the family therapy scene (McGoldrick, 1983) noted that apart from the Women's Project, comprised of Betty Carter, Peggy Papp, Olga Silverstein, and Marianne Walters, there had been only a handful of articles dealing with the subject of women in families and family therapy. Reading the family literature, prior to this time one would hardly know that over a decade of feminism had changed, challenged, and enlarged the very definition of "self" and "family" for countless women and men. Nor would one guess that what happens between a husband and wife in the bedroom or kitchen has something to do with the "rules" of male-female relationships in the broader public sphere.

In contrast to a few lone voices in the late 1970s (Hare-Mustin, 1978), feminist issues have gained increased visibility, attention, and respect. Today, family therapists cannot quite so comfortably ignore the challenge to address the subject of gender in theory, training, and clinical practice (Taggart, 1985). In addition to a growing number of journal articles (see Goldner, 1985), the past few years have witnessed the following: The gathering of some 50 family therapists from around the continent for a Women's Colloquium at Stonehenge, Connecticut in September, 1984 (and again in September, 1986); the publication of the first book on women and family therapy that this conference inspired (Ault-Riché, 1986); the ongoing work of the Women's Project in Family Therapy; the efforts of Monica McGoldrick and others to empower women in our field and facilitate networking; presentations and workshops on the subject of gender issues in family therapy; the appearance of the November/December 1985 issue of the *Family Therapy Networker* focusing on feminist theory and practice; Dorothy Wheeler's formal research project on family therapy and feminism; Harriet Goldhor Lerner's (1985a) book on women's anger which approaches women's relationship problems from a feminist/systemic framework; Bepko and Krestan's (1985) book on alcoholism which includes an exploration of the impact of gender role expectations. These are but a few of many feminist projects that have emerged over the past several years.

Yet despite the steadily growing attempt to make gendered family arrangements a central concern in our work, many family therapists have not responded to the challenge that feminism poses to both theory and practice. Indeed, even "gender sensitive" therapists may not wish to be identified with feminism and continue to view it in a negative light. In a recent issue of the *Family Therapy Networker* (November/December 1986), Richard Meth writes, "The male liberationists and the feminists are extreme examples of groups who believe that their mission is to eliminate flawed gender arrangements. I don't believe membership in one of these groups is necessary for gender sensitivity" (p. 60).

This attitude of condescension, or perhaps simple disinterest, strikes me as odd, for feminist theory and systems theory share common concepts. This is particularly true for Bowen Family Systems Theory. Both feminism and Bowen Theory are primarily concerned with differentiation and clarification of self. Both describe in detail the powerful resistance or "Change Back!" reactions that occur when a de-selfed individual begins to more clearly define the

terms of her own life. Both reject an individual model of psychopathology that locates the problem inside the identified patient.
Both warn of dangers of false dichotomies and polarizations. Both
describe the inseparable nature of the "personal" and the broader
context.

Other schools of family therapy also have significant areas of
conceptual agreement and overlap with feminism, and thus the resistance to dialogue and to serious attempts to integrate the two
theoretical perspectives deserves attention. In 1982, this issue was
raised in the family therapy literature (Libow, Raskin & Caust);
however, these same authors continued to perpetuate the notion that
feminist theory is linear and systems theory is systemic. If one ac-
cepts this premise, attempts to integrate linear and circular concepts
may be dismissed as mere failures to appreciate their differences.

I believe that labeling feminist theory as "linear" and family
systems theory as "circular" creates one more false dichotomy or
polarization that stands in the way of achieving a more in-depth
understanding of human systems. Not only do such labels reflect a
lack of conceptual clarity (i.e., much of feminist theory is circular),
but they may block us from clearly identifying the real differences
between the two theories, which are not primarily epistemological.
For example, while both theories emphasize the inextricably interwoven nature of the individual and the individual's broader context,
feminists define the broader context to include not only the multigenerational family but the societal system as well. Furthermore,
feminists pay considerable attention to this broader context at both
theoretical and· applied levels. *Viewed from feminist eyes, a family
focus that ignores the dysfunction of the sociocultural system is
equally as narrow as an intrapsychic focus on an identified patient
that ignores the primary dysfunction in the family system.* From my
own feminist perspective, systems theory is not contextual or systemic enough.

## NEGLECT OF THE SOCIOCULTURAL SYSTEM

Perhaps the clearest example of the interrelatedness between the
dysfunction of the patriarchal sociocultural system level and the
specific dysfunctional patterns individual families present clinically, is seen in the odd-man-out, child-focused family. The all-too-
familiar dance, repetitively reenacted by the distant husband/father,
the child-focused wife/mother, and the symptomatic child who is
too loyal to grow herself up — is prescribed and perpetuated by the

patriarchal societal system just as this particular type of family organization reinforces and perpetuates that same societal dysfunction. As long as men are the makers and shapers of culture in the world outside the home, as long as women are not free to define the terms of their own lives, as long as society continues to convey the message that mother *is* the child's environment, then the basic dysfunctional triad of distant, overfunctioning father, emotionally intense, overinvolved mother with a child with little room to grow up, is a natural outgrowth and microcosm of the culture. As Goldner (1985) has recently argued, "the archetypal 'family case' of the overinvolved mother and peripheral father is best understood not as a clinical problem, but as the product of a historical process two hundred years in the making" (p. 31).

Family structure and societal structure form a circular, self-perpetuating, downward spiraling cycle (Lerner, 1978). The more women are blocked from proceeding with their own growth and excluded from positions of power and authority outside the home, the more they become excessively child-focused. As emotional intensity and intimacy increase within the mother-child dyad, the distance and emotional isolation of the husband/father becomes more entrenched. In turn, children growing up within this context develop a dread of the "destructive" powers of women and move toward patriarchal solutions of their own, in a defensive attempt to further confine and constrict women's spheres of activity and control in their own adult lives (Lerner, 1974b). These solutions include men's participation in cultural adaptations that restrict avenues of growth and opportunity open to women, the devaluation and disowning of "feminine" aspects of self, as well as women's tacit support for restrictive and oppressive cultural arrangements and their "willingness" to de-self themselves by avoiding and suppressing areas of activity and competence that threaten men. The "solution," of course, only perpetuates the problem. Men can be blamed on the one hand, or the bad mothers who "produced" them on the other; but feminists and systems theorists both might agree that how one punctuates reality is not the primary issue. Rather, the question of greater importance is how to disrupt such cycles, and where to intervene to change the rules.

At the heart of systemic theory is the notion that a dysfunctional *individual* can best be helped by disrupting and changing the rigid rules, expectations, and structures that inhibit growth in the family system. Yet, systems theory has not seriously addressed the parallel notion that dysfunctional *families* can best be helped by disrupting and changing the rigid rules, expectations, and structures of patriarchal culture. On this subject family therapists have tended to maintain a dignified fraternal silence.

## BOWEN THEORY

Bowen Family Systems Theory has been most conspicuous in disregarding the relationship between sex-role prescriptions and the differentiation of self. Indeed, Bowen's Differentiation of Self Scale is a virtual caricature of "feminine" and "masculine" attributes as they are defined and prescribed by culture (Hare-Mustin, 1978). Low on the differentiation scale is the stereotypic female: life energy goes into seeking love, approval, happiness, and security; there is relatively little investment in pursuing independent, goal-directed activities; feelings and emotions override more planful, intellectual (i.e., "masculine") modes of thought; and "being for" others outweighs "being for" the self. Bowen Theory purports to identify those factors which determine an individual's place on the differentiation scale without mentioning the voluminous body of professional literature that demonstrates that females are schooled in undifferentiation (that is, as Bowen himself defines it) from the moment they are first wrapped in a pink blanket (Lerner, 1974a; Miller, 1976). Interestingly, Bowen's description of the poorly differentiated individual is identical to the diagnostic criteria used by psychiatry to define the "hysterical" female, just as the traits and qualities of the well-differentiated individual are those labeled "masculine" by traditional mental health professionals (Lerner, 1974a). I will not speculate on the theoretical implications of these equations, but rather will puzzle over the fact that, by its virtual silence in this area, Bowen Theory denies that sex-role prescriptions and the differing male-female socialization process have any particular implications for the development of dysfunctional patterns in family systems and the difficulties inherent in self-differentiation.

This inattention to cultural sex-role prescriptions is particularly striking in regard to Bowen's ideas about how de-selfed individuals provide their partners with an enhanced sense of "pseudo-self." As Lerner (1983) and Miller (1976) note, de-selfing is culturally prescribed for women, who are taught to strengthen men by containing and expressing the very qualities that men fear in themselves and do not wish to be "weakened" by. De-selfing and underfunctioning are still considered by some to be the hallmarks of successful femininity (Lerner, 1983, 1985a). A number of contemporary books (e.g., Andelin, 1980) coach women on how to actively feign or cultivate weakness, dependency, and childlike vulnerability in order to bolster the male ego and keep the marital relationship intact. Even intellectually liberated women unconsciously fear they will be hurtful or destructive to men if they relinquish an underfunctioning position and exercise more fully their authority and competence. True enough, the old cultural dictates that taught women to "play dumb," "let the man win," and "pretend he's boss" are outdated; however, the underlying message remains an unconscious guiding rule for many women who are taught to strengthen men and safeguard relationships by minimizing or sacrificing their strengths and abilities and by accepting false and confining definitions of self. This rule is that the weaker sex must protect the stronger sex from recognizing the strength of the weaker sex lest the stronger sex feel weakened by the strength of the weaker sex (Lerner, 1983).

Men also learn to de-self themselves in certain areas. Certainly, the pressures on men to overfunction, through relinquishing the experience and expression of dependency, passivity, vulnerability, and other so-called "weaknesses" or "feminine attributes," constitute a de-selfing of its own kind. Further, men are characteristically the underfunctioners when it comes to attunement with the emotional components of human experience, and the ability to rely on cooperative, rather than aggressive/competitive modes of interactions. While it is clear to feminists and systems thinkers alike that underfunctioners and overfunctioners reinforce each other's complimentary positions and "get stuck" in self-perpetuating sequences of interaction that are difficult to interrupt, family systems theorists have yet to pay sufficient attention to the cultural "rules of the game" which effect and reinforce these circular dances. Also they have not seriously examined the ways in which the very structure of work and of family roles (as defined and prescribed by patriarchal culture) block differentiation in women and breed family dysfunction. Here, I agree with the feminist position that differentiation and clarification of self are impossible tasks for women (or men, for that matter) and will be until women collectively change and challenge the constricting and distorting roles, rules, and structures that block their ability to define self and shape culture.[2]

## "But Men are Not to Blame!"
## A Systemic Epistemological Muddle

S. E. Barrows: . . . assessing blame—that's what systems thinkers aren't supposed to do.

M. Selvini Palazzoli: Yes, because this is cultural. Very often, women say their husbands are horrible; men say their wives are terrible. After that, we become aware that this was cultural, that all the husbands and wives were at the same level.

Palazzoli's words (cited in Barrows, 1982) echo the sentiments of other family systems therapists who appear to have little interest in feminism for two reasons: first, this realm of "culture" is of no relevance for by definition, it is to be dismissed; second, the "battle of the sexes" is a war of blaming and blaming, for systems theorists, reflects an epistemological failure to appreciate the circular interrelatedness of all phenomena.

At one level of analysis, I am in full agreement with the systemic position. Every family therapist knows that it is not useful to think in terms of villains and victims in a family system; spouses choose each other for good reasons, provoke and maintain each other's behavior and resist the very changes that they seek. Psychoanalytic theorists also are aware that if one looks deeply enough, no one is to blame for anything. Cause and effect are circularly intertwined and we all do the best we can, given our context and circumstances.

"Blaming," however, is a word used glibly in reference to feminists and has not been clearly enough defined. On the one hand, there is repetitive, nonproductive blaming that only serves to maintain homeostasis and blur one's sense of clarity of self and responsibility for one's own life. On the other hand, there is other-directed anger that occurs when an individual can clearly identify those external forces impeding growth and blocking one's ability to develop the self and define the terms of one's own life. Members of subordinate groups experience this other-directed anger when they are able to see beyond the dominant group's definition of "reality" and clearly identify their own subordinate status. This other-directed anger does not reflect enmeshment or undifferentiation, but rather is an expression of dignity and self-regard which are essential milestones in the process of personal and social change. *Other-directed anger that serves to challenge the status quo must be distinguished from nonproductive anger that serves only to maintain it.*

An example of the failure to make this distinction can be found in Gluck, Dannefer, and Milea's (1980) chapter on "Women in Families'' which appears in Carter and McGoldrick's (1980) book, *The Family Life Cycle*. Here, the authors state that ''. . . the premise that women are victims — of men, of society, of tradition, or whatever — implies total powerlessness and the inability to effect change'' (p. 297). They fail to appreciate that even the most radical feminists do not sit around passively bemoaning their victimized status. To the contrary, a realistic appraisal of one's self or one's group as victimized, oppressed, or subordinate is a prerequisite if women are to speak out effectively and take individual and collective action on their own behalf. Those women who openly express anger about their victimized status are the same women who have been busy writing women back into language and history, discovering women's roots in prior generations, and establishing countless programs and services central to women's lives, such as health clinics, child care centers, antirape squads, scholarly journals, women's studies programs in universities, to name just a few. In many cases, it is the *failure* to identify one's subordinate status, combined with the excessive inhibition of other-directed anger, that leaves individuals and groups powerless to effect change.

The systemic notion that it is epistemologically incorrect for women to blame men because they (women) participate fully in their dilemma, is both accurate and absurd. History books teach us that no dominant group has ever relinquished power voluntarily. Patriarchy does not decline when individual women make clear ''I-statements'' about their thoughts, feelings, and wants. Indeed, it is extremely difficult for subordinate group members to identify their own thoughts, feelings, and wants, because dominant group members define the very nature of things, including the true nature and appropriate place of the subordinate group. Further, no subordinate group has ever protested its own subordination without taking great risks and incurring considerable punishment. It took the better part of a century before women were granted the right to vote, following long years of mass organizing and militant struggle, which included picketing, demonstrations, jailings, and hunger strikes, after more ''ladylike'' tactics failed. During this time, a number of society's prominent experts argued that to grant women equality in this sphere would threaten the fabric of American society and corrupt women's God-given nature. ''Change Back!'' reactions of this order and magnitude are alive and well today, making it extremely difficult for women individually to define self and collectively to identify and protest their own subordinate status.

Most feminists would agree with systems theorists that the question of "who is to blame" is an intellectual puzzle that can be debated forever and is beside the point. I believe, however, that the familiar phrase, "But men are not to blame!" (while true at one level) functions as a countermove or "Change Back!" reaction to silence female anger and maintain the status quo in the face of the powerful anxiety that is inevitably stirred when a subordinate or de-selfed group insists on more clearly defining the terms of their own lives. Surely, the differentiation of self in subordinate group members is not facilitated when their anger and frustration is disqualified by arguing that no one is to blame for anything, or that its expression itself denotes a lack of epistemological clarity.

## A MATTER OF VALUES

The very term "feminist therapist" seems to conjure up images of family therapists who go about imposing their values on clients and families at the expense of both therapeutic neutrality and men. What is remarkable about this criticism is the implicit assumption that non-feminist therapists do not have values, beliefs, and biases that shape their therapeutic work and effect their differential reactions to each sex. As I have argued elsewhere, there is no value-free therapy (Lerner, 1982, 1985b). The questions we do or do not ask, the interventions we make or fail to think of, what we choose to focus on or to ignore—all these reflect our deep seated and often unexamined assumptions about what is natural, appropriate, and functional for each sex. Or, as Betty Carter (1985) puts it, "You cannot *not* act out of your age, gender, sibling position, experience, belief system and wisdom, or lack of it. Your only choice is whether to do this consciously or unconsciously" (p. 78).

Still, it is not surprising that feminists are viewed as uniquely biased or as having an ax to grind. It is in the nature of human nature that the dominant group culture experiences their view of reality as the "objective" or correct one against which alternate views are judged deviant. Viewing the world through a patriarchal lens is equated with a position of "neutrality" requiring neither explanation nor justification, while those of us operating from a feminist perspective are suspected of bias or excessive subjectivity. The following example from a brief consultation illustrates this point.

## Dr. B and the Porters

Dr. B worked with Mr. and Mrs. Porter for seven months before requesting consultation on this case. Mr. Porter was a middle management executive and Mrs. Porter was a homemaker with a college degree. Both were in their early 40s with three daughters, ages 6, 12, and 14. Dr. B described a marital situation seen commonly in clinical work: the wife blamed her husband for her unhappiness yet she implicitly complied with his demands. She was unable to move from ineffective complaining to assertive claiming and although she angered easily, she did not make moves to effectively challenge the status quo. In addition she was excessively reactive to her husbands work problems, and according to Dr. B, she placed her husband in a "double bind." If Mr. Porter did not provide his wife with a full report on what was happening at work, she felt angry and rejected. When he did fill her in she would either move in quickly to advise or fix things, or she would criticize his management of or reactions to a particular situation. When stress was high, Mr. Porter occasionally threatened divorce.

Dr. B, who was learning to work from a Bowen Family Systems framework, sought my help because he felt unsuccessful in helping the wife assume a calmer, more objective, and less blaming perspective in the marriage. In addition, he found himself blaming the blamer (i.e., Mrs. Porter), despite his own attempts to remain neutral and to assume a systemic perspective. While Dr. B was aware that Mrs. Porter, like most wives, overfunctioned enormously on the domestic scene at her own expense, he nonetheless felt put off by what he labeled as manipulative and passive-aggressive behavior. For example, Mrs. Porter reported feeling resentful about her husband's practice of giving her an "allowance" and asking her to account for her personal expenses. But rather than taking a firm and nonnegotiable stand that this was not acceptable to her, Mrs. Porter "manipulated" her husband into giving her extra money which she then spent irresponsibly and impulsively.

Using the genograms that he had constructed during initial meetings, Dr. B had questioned Mr. and Mrs. Porter about the history of marriage in the previous generations, including questions about how marital partners got along, how money was managed, how differences were navigated, and so forth. Dr. B's primary goal in working from a multigenerational model was to help Mrs. Porter to separate or differentiate from her "maschochistic" mother which he hoped, in turn, would allow her to move out of her angry, dependent position in the marriage.

What Dr. B had ignored entirely however, was the impact on this marriage of the wife's economic dependency. That Mrs. Porter was one husband away from a welfare check, and that she had no life plan or personal goals for herself was a subject matter that Dr. B had neither thought about nor explored in marital therapy. This "traditional" family structure was simply the norm for Dr. B and did not, in itself, suggest any particular arena for questioning.

During our consultation hour Dr. B requested that we focus on Mrs. Porter who was the source of his distress. To this end, I asked him to think about any number of questions:

Was there a connection between Mrs. Porter's overinvolvement with her husband's work problems and her own lack of participation in the work world outside the home? Did she believe her husband's work to be more valuable than her own, and if so, was this a factor in her "wishy-washy" approach to asking him to take on more housework and child-care? What was the connection, if any, between Mrs. Porter's irresponsible and manipulative behavior around her "allowance" and her actual financial dependence?

Which women in Mrs. Porter's nuclear and extended family had clarified personal and work goals for themselves and which women had not? For those women in the previous generations who had put their energy into their own life goals, how did this impact on their marriage? How did Mrs. Porter's sister, mother, and grandmother balance responsibility for family with responsibility for self? Had Mrs. Porter ever talked with these women about their personal goals and aspirations or the lack of them? Did Mrs. Porter think about long-term goals for self?

How could we understand the fact that Mrs. Porter whined and complained about her circumstances, but did not effectively clarify a bottom line position with her husband on any major emotional issue (e.g., "This allowance business is not acceptable to me. I also work, albeit in the home, and I want the same access to our finances that you have")? What specifically did she think would happen in this marriage if she began to operate from a position of greater strength and assertiveness? Did Mrs. Porter believe she had to choose between having a marriage and having a self?

If her marriage ended in divorce (as do almost 50% of marriages), what was Mrs. Porter's life plan? Was she familiar with the statistics regarding the economic status of women with dependent

children following divorce? Did Mrs. Porter equate divorce not
only with the loss of her primary relationship, but also with the loss
of status, identity, esteem, and financial support? If Mrs. B believed that she could not survive economically without her marriage, how did this effect her ability to navigate clearly and assert-
ively within it? Is it possible to assume a truly differentiated
position in a marital or work system if one is convinced that one
cannot live without it?

Did Mrs. Porter view her gender as having some relevance to her
current problems and unhappiness? Did she see other women (both
on her genogram and outside the family) struggling with issues similar to her own? Had she connected with any of these persons to
share perspectives on common problems and to learn how other
women had attempted to solve similar dilemmas? In what way did
the past decade and a half of feminism influence, or not influence,
her thinking about herself and her family?

Dr. B had not considered most of the above questions which he
pondered with interest. Yet he reacted negatively to the idea that we
might think together about opening up related lines of questioning
within the marital sessions, while staying relevant to the couples
presenting problems. Dr. B had chosen to consult with me in part
because of my knowledge of women's issues, yet he now feared his
therapeutic neutrality was at stake. "I think any questions along
these lines would convey that Mrs. Porter should get a job or become more liberated. I'm just not comfortable imposing values on
clients." Dr. B told me that the consultation had nonetheless been
very helpful to him because his angry reactions toward Mrs. Porter
were replaced by more empathic ones, as my questions led him to
consider more thoughtfully the context of her life. Yet he could not
see his way clear to translate what he had gained from this consultation into his practice.

Like Dr. B, I do not view it as a therapist's job to encourage a
client to seek employment, embrace feminism, or the like. In working from a Bowen perspective, I use questioning to lower intensity,
to broaden a client's perspective and sense of connectedness to her
own family and cultural context, to encourage thinking and the
gathering of facts, and to help her view as many options as possible
with the greatest degree of clarity and objectivity. Surely women
have enough "experts" telling them what to do. What was interesting to me about Dr. B's position, however, was his assumption that
*not* opening up certain areas for questioning, and *failing* to focus on

certain aspects of context represented a neutral or objective stance. From my perspective, Dr. B's absorption of patriarchal values regarding "traditional" family structure stood in the way of his becoming a more skilled questioner and ultimately a more helpful therapist to this couple.

## CONCLUDING REMARKS

Obviously, family therapists need not be agents of social change. By failing to address the broader patriarchal context, however, systems theorists are akin to physicians who are highly skilled in treating individual coal-miners with black lung disease but somehow overlook the fact that the conditions of the mines contribute to the incidence of the problem and are also an appropriate, if not essential, locus of change. Not every person who works down in the mines will contract black lung disease, and not everyone will become visibly sick from the patriarchy. But one still might ask, "Why the silence?" (See Wheeler, 1985; Goldner, 1985.) Surely the failure to focus on the broader societal picture creates any number of decidedly unsystemic dichotomies; the dichotomy between the personal and the political, the dichotomy between family and culture, the dichotomy between systems theory and feminist theory. Feminism, in contrast, argues that "The personal is political," and rejects the notion that family dysfunction can be understood without thoroughly examining the meanings and implications of patriarchal systems which give form and shape to the family and to the very process of differentiation of self.

Exploring the interrelationships between patriarchal society and the mechanisms of family systems is a complex and difficult task, precisely because patriarchy shapes our very sense of reality. As the physicist Fritjof Capra (1982) notes:

> The power of patriarchy has been extremely difficult to understand because it is all-pervasive. It has influenced our most basic ideas about human nature and about our relation to the universe — "man's" nature and "his" relation to the universe, in patriarchal language. It is the one system which, until recently, had never in recorded history been openly challenged, and whose doctrines were so universally accepted that they seemed to be laws of nature. (p. 29)

Capra (although not a family therapist) is one systems theorist who truly appreciates the relevance of feminist theory to the understanding of all systems. Rather than labeling feminism as "linear," he notes that it is profoundly ecological in its visions and its modes of thought, and he concludes that "the Feminist Movement is one of the strongest cultural currents of our time and will have a profound effect on our further evolution" (p. 29).

Understandably it is tempting to avoid attending to the patriarchal system in which the family is embedded, for the consequences of patriarchal structure have become so devastatingly apparent. Today, one issue that confronts the American family is more pressing than all others and that issue is survival. No longer can we count on the continuity of future generations, or even on the survival of our own children into adulthood. Family systems theorists can make a special contribution toward understanding the run-away symmetrical process characterizing the nuclear arms race if we are courageous enough to make this our business. And when the survival of all families hangs by a thread, how can it not be? As a feminist, I am well aware of how difficult it is to direct serious and steady attention to subjects that disturb our sense of serenity and emotional calm. Yet, our commitment to understanding and helping families can only suffer when we are unable to address larger systems issues which shape the family and are, of necessity, controversial and painful.

## NOTES

1. Interestingly, Bowen is one of the few family therapists who has attempted to apply his ideas to societal processes, although his politics are viewed by his critics as remarkably right wing (Debra Leupnitz, in press). As I understand it, Bowen views feminist protest, (along with other forms of social activism) as an emotionally reactive position, reflective of both individual immaturity and societal regression, that leads us down the nonproductive path of linear thinking (i.e., blaming men) and the relinquishing of responsibility for self. That Dr. Bowen's societal analysis renders invisible issues of gender inequality and that he ignores or negatively connotes feminist concerns is hardly remarkable. Of greater interest is the fact that within the Georgetown Family Center there appears to be neither dissent nor expressions of differences regarding feminism. With the exception of one explicitly antifeminist book to come out of the Bowen group (Hall, 1979) it is as if the past 15 years of feminism have simply not occurred.

2. In actual clinical practice, I find Bowen's work to be the most congruent with my feminist values and beliefs of all individual and family perspectives. For

a discussion of the parallels between applied Bowen theory and feminism, see Lerner, 1985b.

# REFERENCES

Andelin, H. (1980). *Fascinating Womanhood*. New York: Bantam.

Ault-Riché, M. (1986). *Women and Family Therapy*. Rockville, MD: Aspen Systems Corporation.

Barrows, S. E. (1982). Interview with Maura Selvini Palazzoli and Guiliana Prata. *American Journal of Family Therapy, 10*, 60-69.

Bepko, C. & Krestan, K. (1985). *The Responsibility Trap*. New York: The Free Press.

Bowen, M. (1978). *Family Therapy in Clinical Practice*. New York: Jason Aronson.

Capra, F. (1982). *The Turning Point*. New York: Simon & Schuster.

Carter, B. (1985). Ms intervention's guide to "correct" feminist family therapy. *The Family Therapy Networker, 9*, 78-79.

Gluck, N. R., Dannefer, E. & Milea, K. (1980). Women in Families, in E. A. Carter & M. McGoldrick (Eds.), *Family Life Cycle* (pp. 295-327). New York: Gardner Press, Inc.

Goldner, V. (1985). Feminism and family therapy. *Family Process, 24*, 31-47.

Hall, C. M. (1979). *Women Unliberated*. New York: Hemisphere Publications.

Hare-Mustin, R. (1978). A feminist approach to family therapy. *Family Process, 17*, 181-194.

Kerr, M. E. (1981). Family Systems Theory and Therapy, in A. S. Gurman & D. P. Kniskern (Eds.), *Handbook of Family Therapy*. New York: Brunner Mazel.

Lerner, H. (1974a). The hysterical personality: A woman's disease. *Comprehensive Psychiatry, 15*, 157-164.

Lerner, H. (1974b). Early origins of envy and devaluation of women: Implications for sex role stereotypes. *Bulletin of the Menninger Clinic. 38*, 538-553.

Lerner, H. (1978). On the comfort of patriarchal solutions: Some reflections on Brown's paper. *Journal of Personality and Social Systems*, *1*, 47-50.

Lerner, H. (1982). Special Issues for Women in Psychotherapy. In *The Woman Patient*, Vol. 3, M. Notman & C. Nadelson (Eds.). New York: Plenum.

Lerner, H. (1983). Female dependency in context: Some theoretical and technical considerations. *American Journal of Orthopsychiatry*, *53*, 697-705.

Lerner, H. G. (1985a). *The Dance of Anger*. New York: Harper & Row.

Lerner, H. G. (1985b). Can a feminist still like Murray Bowen. *The Family Therapy Networker, 9*, 36-39.

Libow, J. A., Raskin, T. A. & Caust, B. L. (1982). Feminist and family systems therapy: Are they irreconcilable? *American Journal of Family Therapy, 10*, 3-12.

Luepnitz, D. (in press). *Feminism and Family Therapy*. New York: Basic Books.

McGoldrick, M. (1983). Book review of *The Woman Patient* (1982) Vol. 2 and Vol. 3, M. Notman & C. Nadelson (Eds.), AFTA *Newsletter, 14*, 13-14.

Miller, J. B. (1976). *Toward a New Psychology of Women*. Boston: Beacon Press.

Taggart, M. (1985). The feminist critique in epistemological perspective: Questions of context in family therapy. *Journal of Marital and Family Therapy, 11*, 113-126.

Wheeler, D. (1985). Fear of feminism in family therapy. *The Family Therapy Networker, 9*, 53-55.

Wheeler, D. (research in progress). Defining the parameters of a feminist or gender-sensitive approach to family therapy. Purdue University, Department of Child Development and Family Studies.

Women's Project in Family Therapy (1982). "Mothers and Daughters," Monograph Ser. 1.

Women's Project in Family Therapy (1983). "Mothers and Sons, Fathers and Daughters," Monograph Ser. 2.

# Enmeshment, Fusion or Relatedness?
## A Conceptual Analysis

### Michele Bograd

**SUMMARY.** Basic family systems concepts may reflect prototypically male standards of self and relationships, which contribute to
the common practice of labeling women's preferred interactional
styles as pathological or dysfunctional. Possible biases in the definition and/or application of the terms "enmeshment" and "fusion"
are elucidated through examination of gender differences in individual development, of the socially determined structure of the contemporary family, and of the social context of inequality. Following
redefinition and validation of women's relational skills, implications
for theory are briefly discussed.

The terms "enmeshment" and "fusion" are such basic family
systems terms that many family therapists, regardless of their theoretical persuasion, employ them as descriptive of dysfunctional
family structures and processes. A primary archetype of family
therapy is the triad of enmeshed mother, disengaged father, and
symptomatic child. As systemic-organizational constructs, these
terms are ostensibly gender-neutral — yet more women than men are
labeled "fused." Although it has been suggested that the feminist
critique of family therapy extends into the theoretical or epistemological domains (Goldner, 1985c; James, 1985; James & McIntyre,
1983; Taggart, 1985), no articles to date have systematically examined specific family systems constructs from a woman-based perspective. This article will suggest directions for this work through a
beginning conceptual analysis of the related basic family therapy
terms of enmeshment and fusion.

Michele Bograd, PhD, a Psychologist, is in private practice in Cambridge,
MA. She is on the faculties of the Kantor Family Institute (Somerville, MA) and
of the Family Institute of Cambridge, and is an instructor on psychiatry at Harvard
Medical School. Correspondence may be addressed to 50 Chauncey St., Water-
town, MA 02172.

The analysis rests on the premises that: (1) basic family therapy constructs are male-defined and do not adequately address gender differences in human development or the socially constructed conditions of family life; (2) criteria of healthy system functioning reflect stereotypically male characteristics; (3) assessed by these standards, the preferred interpersonal styles of women are judged as undesirable or pathogenic; (4) although a distinguishing criterion of family therapy is its emphasis on relationships and interactional patterns, family therapy lacks a language of connection and intimacy (Bernal & Ysern, 1986; Layton, 1984; Luepnitz, 1984; Women's Project, 1982); and (5) the positive description of prototypically female experiences can provide new metaphors for enriching systems models.

## *WHY IS THE STUDY OF LANGUAGE IMPORTANT?*

Feminist theorists have demonstrated that language is "man-made" (Spender, 1980): our cultural system of meanings and symbols reifies prototypically male views of the world as normative, positive standards. In contrast, the experiences of women are defined as other, as different, as deviant, or as deficient. Men and women do not stand in the same relationship to language. Since many of women's experiences are not positively encoded linguistically, they are distorted and/or rendered invisible. Language is not simply descriptive but prescriptive: as we narrate an event, we imply what should be.

What relevance does this have for family therapists? Drawing from the sciences of biology and cybernetics, family systems theory appears objective, scientific, and neutral. But careful examination of our terms reveals that the technical organizational language of systems theory can highlight male-defined realities (Bograd, 1984, 1986a; Spender, 1980), ignore or distort women's experiences (Women's Project in Family Therapy, 1982, 1983), and smuggle in biased content (Bograd, 1986b, 1986c; Goldner, 1985a; James, 1985; James & McIntyre, 1983). Since clinical theory provides the direction for clinical intervention, these concerns are not simply esoteric but inherently practical and political. It is incumbent upon feminist family therapists to analyze how linguistic accounts are employed in family therapy and to what ends (Taggart, 1985) and to develop constructs that validate prototypically female experiences.

The goal is not to glorify women, but to broaden our language and so our understandings of the variety of human experiences.

Several steps comprise a feminist analysis of family therapy constructs and theories: (1) scrutinizing terms for biases against women, especially regarding how healthy functioning is defined and how adequately gender differences and the social context of inequality are taken into account; (2) describing and validating women's experiences in families, which current models distort, pathologize, or render invisible; (3) detailing how gender influences family interactional sequences and impasses, through sensitive examination of the experiential worlds of men and women and careful operationalization of the vicissitudes of prototypically male and female ways of being; (4) expanding systems models to capture how male/female relations are shaped and constrained by the complex interrelationships of intrapsychic factors, interactional processes, family structures and societal variables; and (5) developing new metaphors and models of family relations that are truly gender-free—that is, equally applicable to both men and women and descriptive of the range and diversity of all human capacities.

Although such a comprehensive effort is beyond the scope of this paper, this preliminary analysis of the terms "enmeshment" and "fusion" will address how their definitions and uses contain biases against women, and will begin positively connoting women's experiences that are currently perceived as pathogenic or dysfunctional.

## FUSION AND ENMESHMENT

The terms fusion and enmeshment derive from two distinct theoretical models: Bowen Family Systems Theory and Structural Family Therapy. Bowen (1971; 1978) developed a linear model of healthy human development. On one end of the continuum is fusion. The fused individual has no clear sense of self and is governed by feelings and intuitions rather than by a consistent system of rational beliefs and opinions. Because of poor self/other boundaries, he or she is too oriented to relationships, to responding to the needs of others, and to seeking approval. In contrast stands the abstract ideal of the differentiated self. Because of clear ego boundaries, the individual achieves relative separation of emotion and intellect and so is motivated by reason and logic, rather than by intense feelings or relationship demands. Acting autonomously, the fully differentiated person is not a solitary individualist but tolerates both intimacy and isolation. A major goal of Bowen Family Systems interventions is to help individual family members "rise up out of the emotional togetherness binding us all."

Enmeshment is defined somewhat differently. As defined in Minuchin's early works (1974; 1981), structural family therapy rests on a curvilinear model of adaptive functioning: boundaries between subsystems can be too rigid or too diffuse. Enmeshed families, in which individual autonomy is sacrificed for the sake of connection, are characterized by blurred boundaries and low interpersonal distance leading to overinvolvement, extreme sensitivity, and acute reactivity between family members. But too rigid boundaries lead to disengagement: too great interpersonal distance between individuals and subsystems results in limited potential for "reverberation" or responsiveness and in the relative absence of emotional connection, warmth, and support. Interdependence is the ideal. Boundaries are clear enough to allow individual members to carry out functions without interference but permeable enough to permit contact and the flow of information. While promoting the experience of self as a separate whole, structural family therapists equally emphasize the importance of mutuality and reciprocity between part and context, between individual and the family system.

## BIASES IN DEFINITIONS
## AND APPLICATION OF TERMS

Since many family therapists use the terms enmeshment and fusion interchangeably, the distinctions between them will be collapsed in this article. Although these terms were developed to objectively describe systems, in practice they contain biases against women. While popular use may have distorted their original theoretically grounded meanings (Minuchin, personal communication, 1986), the biases may also be intrinsic to their definitions. As abstract technical terms describing parts of a system regardless of gender, these constructs may pathologize women's differential individual development, particularize family relations that have broader social determinants, and minimize the consequences of male/female inequality.

## Male-Defined Standards of Mental Health

The "neutral" standards of mental health and human development often reflect prototypically male characteristics (Broverman, Broverman, Clarkson, Rosenkrantz & Vogel, 1970; Gilligan, 1982). This is most evident in Bowen's model, in which qualities defined as adaptive for the system are stereotypical male traits writ large: rationality, autonomy, detachment, individuality, independence. Assessments of healthy functioning are inversely related to the degree of fusion. The problem is not that certain "male" characteristics are valued, but that they are located on a bipolar continuum that devalues or pathologizes stereotypically female qualities of emotionality, need for intense connection, and investment in relationships (Hare-Mustin, 1978, 1980; Layton, 1984; Lerner, 1983; Women's Project in Family Therapy, 1982).

At first glance, structural family therapy appears exempt from this bias, since enmeshment and disengagement are technically descriptive of preferred family transactional styles and are not linked to qualitative differences between functional and dysfunctional systems (Minuchin, 1974). Although both extreme female qualities (enmeshment) and extreme male qualities (disengagement) are defined as maladaptive, "enmeshment" evokes stronger critical reactions than "disengagement" and means different things depending on whether it is applied to men or to women. The greater negative connotations of enmeshment may be due to the fact that it describes stereotypically female qualities, reflecting the linguistic rule of the semantic derogation of women: words primarily associated with women become pejorative (Jordan, 1983; Spender, 1980; Stiver, 1984).

The idealization of the male self as a standard for human development and healthy system functioning poses another profound dilemma. Given the structure of current family relations in which mothers as primary caretakers have different relationships with their sons and daughters, men and women may experience the self and relationships in qualitatively different ways and use different criteria by which to make moral judgments (Chodorow, 1978; Dinnerstein, 1976; Gilligan, 1982). If this is so, male-defined standards of adaptive functioning are not relevant for women. If the male represents the positive, the female, by definition, becomes negative (Spender, 1980). Yet family therapists cannot address the question of whether men and women have equivalent capacities and desires to achieve autonomy, differentiation and clear subsystem boundaries. Given their conceptual commitment to focus solely on current transactional patterns, family therapists usually ignore the gender and developmental history of the individual components of a system (Layton, 1984).

### Blaming the Woman

Lacking a positive language of connection and intimacy (Bernal & Ysern, 1985; Layton, 1984; Luepnitz, 1984; Women's Project, 1982) family therapists label a wide range of women's behaviors as enmeshment or fusion. If a woman is emotional, intensely involved with her family, and attentive to nonverbal cues, this constellation of behaviors is negatively defined as overcontrolling, intrusive, and demanding. Holding the individual woman accountable for the dysfunctional patterns of the entire family system is a major sexist bias of family therapy (Bograd, 1984, 1986a, 1986b, 1986c; Goldner, 1985a, 1985c; Hare-Mustin, 1978, 1980; Jacobson, 1983; James & McIntyre, 1983; Women's Project, 1982). Two conceptual errors perpetuate this bias: (1) confusing a term descriptive of the system with fixed individual traits of one of its parts; and (2) pathologizing the normative structure of family relations.

Enmeshment describes a transactional pattern between two or more individuals. But family therapists often refer to the enmeshed mother out of context, implying that she has blurred boundaries creating problems in the entire family system. Since most mothers have intense connections to their spouses and children, labeling such connection "fused" or "enmeshed" punishes women for making interpersonal affiliations central in their lives. This is not simply ameliorated by broadening a formulation to encompass all parts of the system, since formulations can punctuate behavioral sequences to emphasize the influence of one family member—typically the mother or wife. A common formulation reads: Mother fuses with daughter, excluding father from the family. As systemic language cloaks linear explanation, circular causality or recursiveness gives way to blaming the woman.

Technically, terms like enmeshment or fusion should connote a specific constellation of transactional sequences that deviate from normal family processes in ways that lead to symptomatic behavior. But if the structures and processes currently labeled enmeshment are standard features of the typical contemporary family, then it is erroneous to label them as pathogenic or dysfunctional. Although systems theory suggests that the family is embedded in and reciprocally related to the larger social context, most family therapists tend to focus on the nuclear family as a relatively closed system. Enmeshment is described as an intrafamilial interpersonal event, which privatizes the family and ascribes responsibility to individual family members for their transactional patterns (Goldner, 1985a; James & McIntyre, 1983; Lerner, 1983; Margolin et al., 1983).

The picture changes, however, as the scope of analysis is broadened. Following the Industrial Revolution, the private and public domains became separate but not equal. With the sexual division of labor, women were relegated to the home to provide the devalued but socially necessary resources of nurturance and care-taking. The structural segregation and unequal power relationships of men and women were supported and rationalized through culturally constructed ideologies of gender, sex roles, and the constructs of "mother" and "father." Thus the contemporary family form is structured in ways that insure the centrality and overinvolvement of women in families and the relatively more peripheral and instrumental orientation of men (James & McIntyre, 1983; Goldner, 1985a, 1985c). Yet when women successfully fulfill their culturally defined and socially regulated roles, they are individually pathologized through labels such as enmeshment. With this, a social fact is mistaken for a clinical disturbance (Goldner, 1985a).

## DOES THE MAP FIT THE TERRITORY? THE MYSTIFICATION OF FAMILY EXPERIENCE

Clinical wisdom suggests that women are labeled enmeshed more frequently than men. While it is undeniable that men and women differ in relational styles, great overlap exists between genders with respect to traits such as objectivity, emotionality, independence, and sensitivity. As we freeze the flow of human interaction through the label "enmeshed wife/disengaged husband," it is important co carefully examine the interrelationship of language and "reality." Do our terms merely simplify transactional patterns or distort them?

Feminist therapists have suggested that the terms with which we encode family life may mystify, not illuminate, family relations (Rubin, 1983). Combining Bowen and Family Systems Theory with a feminist analysis of sex role socialization, Lerner (1983) provides a reformulation of female dependency (read fusion or enmeshment). She suggests that although women act dependently, they often have a fully differentiated strong self, which is camouflaged for the sake of other family members, particularly the husband. "[T]he weaker sex must protect the stronger sex from recognizing the strength of the weaker sex lest the stronger sex feel weakened by the strength of the weaker sex" (Lerner, 1983, p. 701). Eichenbaum and Orbach (1983) state the case more strongly: the belief that women are too dependent, fused, or enmeshed is false. In reality, women are not dependent enough because they assume they need to take care of others without having their own needs met in return. It is men who are dependent on women and who expect to have their needs met and gratified without ever having to acknowledge them—which is denied by husbands, wives and society-at-large.

Since family therapists are sensitive observers of human interaction, how can we account for this obfuscation? The systems terminology influencing how we perceive and encode family life draws from the language and gender stereotypes of the dominant male culture. In a context of inequality, the subordinate group becomes the receptacle of traits denied by the dominant culture, such as dependency or emotionality. Because these traits threaten the dominant group, they are encoded in ways that devalue or minimize them. Through these processes of projection and attribution, society is able to preserve its contradictory features (Joslyn, 1982; Miller, 1976).

The dominant group further maintains its superiority by categorizing and stereotyping subordinates in ways that keep them in their place. Attention is deflected away from the consequences of domination by describing subordinates as morally weak, naturally substandard, or less than human (Miller, 1976). For example, when a woman is labeled enmeshed, family therapists can ignore how her financial dependence on her husband constrains her freedom, how available social options limit her means of personal development, how fear of male violence curtails her activities, and how social reactions constrain her efforts to transform her role. As participants in the dominant culture, family therapists can unwittingly employ available socially constructed realities of men and women in families (James, 1985; Taggart, 1985), without awareness of the political function served by oversimplified descriptions of the inherent paradoxical complexity of male/female relations (Goldner, 1985a; 1985c).

## PRELIMINARY THEORETICAL REFORMULATIONS: ENMESHMENT OF RELATEDNESS?

Given these biases in the definition and application of the terms enmeshment and fusion, should they be discarded? With careful definition, they may have continued utility as long as they are employed with sensitivity to the dimensions of gender and social inequality. As abstract organizational terms, they provide rich insights into family systems features that may indeed be empirically associated with maladaptability or symptomatology. Since any systems definition of pathology first requires elaboration of healthy interactional patterns, it is premature to reach conclusions about the viability of these constructs until family therapists more adequately illuminate and understand the variety of women's experiences. Without such description, family therapists will continue to label prototypically female interactional patterns as deficient (rather than simply as different) and to attribute maladaptive aspects of these patterns to individual women (rather than to familial or social constraints).

To these ends, women must find their own voices, which poses a profound challenge. Out of necessity, we can only employ the gendered male-constructed language of our society. Certain ways of understanding women's experiences are so embedded in our language and in our culturally constituted categories of thought that it is very difficult (even for women) to suspend judgment in order to re-cognize, illuminate, and positively connote women's relational styles (Surrey, 1984). But it is essential to constructively define women's strengths, particularly as they are shaped by our individual development, our family roles, and our location in the social context.

### Individual Development: Female Experiences of Self and Others

It has been argued that family therapists implicitly employ male-defined criteria of individuation and separation as standards of the adaptive functioning of individuals and systems. In male-defined models, autonomy and connection, individuation and belonging are defined as mutually exclusive constructs. There is theoretical evidence that suggests, however, that this model is not appropriate for understanding women's development, specifically their experience of self and relationships (Jordan, 1983; Miller, 1976, 1984; Stiver, 1984; Surrey, 1983, 1984).

Because of the quality of the mother-daughter bond, women's primary experience of the self is relational. The self develops and is validated through a reciprocal process of understanding and empathy, in which mutual connectedness and empowering the other leads to further articulation of the self. Within this context, women develop complex skills. Highly developed cognitive and emotional capacities facilitate their sensitivity to the emotional nuances and needs of others. This requires a strong sense of self characterized by flexible self/other boundaries, permitting intense closeness or caring distance depending on the momentary needs of the other and/or on the situational context. Relying on emotion as well as on reason, women have the capacity to tolerate and express a wide range of feelings, which facilitate identification with others. Demonstrating high adaptability to the short-term or developmental needs of others, women demonstrate a positive capacity to maintain relationships—a process requiring the ability to tolerate the ambiguous manifestations of change.

Individual growth for women does not necessitate diluting intense relationships or disconnecting from the system. On the contrary, for women, the self develops *within* a context of relatedness, not by separating from it. Other aspects of the self (such as autonomy, competence, and self-esteem) become articulated through relational experiences of mutual empathy. The mature self—characterized by complexity and fluidity—co-exists with intense affective connectedness. The goal for women is growth and differentiation within relational systems "where both or all people involved are encouraged and challenged to maintain connection and to foster, adapt and change with the growth of the other" (Surrey, 1984, p. 8).

From this perspective, intense and pervasive interpersonal connectedness is not necessarily dysfunctional. Women's preferred transactional styles (now denigrated as enmeshed or fused) are redefined as complex, highly developed relational skills and capacities. Women's primary need for attachment is not equivalent to pathological dependency; the desire for intense emotional connection is not equivalent to fusion; and responsiveness to others given a fluid but substantial self is not equivalent to poor or nonexistent boundaries.

## Women and Family Roles: Mothering as Activity

Given the premises of most systems models, family therapists rarely analyze the family as a historically situated social institution. Terms such as enmeshment deflect attention from the culturally prescribed and socially structured determinants of women's centrality in families (Goldner, 1985b). The denigration of mothers and of mothering reflects how nurturance and caretaking are devalued by our culture, even as society requires these functions for survival. In fact, mothering is often defined as "doing nothing," as something that comes "naturally" to women—not as work requiring creative and complex skills.

In order to mother capably, women develop an intricate constellation of highly sophisticated interpersonal capacities, including the exquisite sensitivity to the often unspoken, subtle, emotional, and physical needs of others; the ability to note, retain, and organize the voluminous and diverse details of the daily lives of the family members; and the capacity to simultaneously attend to a variety of distinctly separate activities. Constant availability to others requires delaying gratification, being immediately emotionally present, and tolerating continuous interruptions and demands. Fueled by a deep sense of interpersonal responsibility, mothers attempt to balance the often conflicting demands and needs of others, relying on an ethos of care and connectedness (Gilligan, 1982; Goldner, 1985b). Promoting and maintaining complicated, multidimensional, intense family involvements presupposes a relatively strong sense of self with highly developed cognitive, emotional, and interpersonal capacities.

While this may seem self-evident, it is important to remember that terms such as "enmeshment" highlight only the presumed failures of mothering. Family therapy lacks terms that encode the taken-for-granted strengths, skills, and capacities of women as they engage in the complex activity of mothering.

## The Social Context: The Hidden Strengths of the Subordinate Class

The previous analysis of the socially structured inequality between men and women in families and in the larger society reveals that activities and qualities devalued by the dominant group are relegated to subordinates and encoded in ways that render subordinates defective, immature, or dysfunctional. But in a context of inequality, the subordinate group must develop certain skills to insure survival. First, women must acquire superior relational skills to protect and maintain their connection to men who wield symbolic or actual power over them. Since the dominant class tends to deny its vulnerabilities and weaknesses, subordinates develop great sensitivity to nonverbal cues, to what is not spoken. Members of the dominant group don't need to develop capacities for relation and connection, because it is assumed they will be cared for by subordinates.

Second, since the dominant group creates language and controls material resources, the subordinate group exists in an alien environment. The subordinates need to learn all about the dominant culture in order to survive—requiring the ability to recognize and tolerate difference, to translate across cultures, and to master the rules of a different game (Schaef, 1981). Again, this relationship is asymmetrical, since the dominant group can exploit the services of subordinates, without sensitivity to their distinctive culture. For this reason, the dominant group is often threatened when subordinates begin to name and so legitimize their own experiences and values as this challenges the status quo and reveals the weaknesses and vulnerabilities of the more powerful group.

## IMPLICATIONS FOR CURRENT FAMILY SYSTEMS THEORIES

Highlighting and valuing women's relational abilities is not simply an exercise in positive connotation or strategic reframing. The act of naming and so legitimating the origin and nature of women's interpersonal patterns challenges family therapists to develop terms that adequately capture the experiences of both men and women in families. Every family therapy model rests on a metaphor of relationships, regardless of how explicitly it is acknowledged and described. Popular metaphors are relatively mechanistic (Luepnitz, 1984): the focus on power, control, hierarchy, authority, and individuality reflects a view of family members as "commodities in a market-economy of relationships" (Bernal & Ysern, 1986, p. 132). It is paradoxical that family therapists, sophisticated in understanding systems and relational patterns, lack a language of attachment and intimacy (Layton, 1984; Women's Project in Family Therapy, 1982). Yet the development of such a language need not start from scratch. The family therapy literature already contains certain concepts, such as interdependency (Minuchin, 1974), that speak to the complex interplay in human systems of self and other, separation and connection. But it will also be necessary to begin developing different metaphors of relationships. The positive examination of women's experiences suggests new vocabularies for family therapy, which may ultimately influence the structure and goals of clinical interventions.

The effort to validate prototypically female transactional patterns does not deny that they have maladaptive components or manifestations. But the continued use of terms describing the dangers or vicissitudes of intense attachment first requires careful analysis of the normal, growth-promoting, and system-maintaining components of women's relational styles. After terms denoting dysfunction are carefully operationalized, family systems formulations must clearly establish (and not simply assume) the systemic links between symptomatology of a family member and the relational style of the wife or mother. As efforts are made to clarify and limit the use of terms that inappropriately pathologize women's intense emotional connectedness, we must expand our repertoire of terms describing the failure of attachment. Although family therapists can easily categorize forms of "too much" relational connection, few words point to its relative absence. For example, "disengagement" does not adequately capture the complexity of relationships between men and their families nor how men's willingness or ability to be intensely interrelated with others is shaped by internal, familial, normative, and cultural constraints.

But the assessment of the relational capacities of men and women in families presupposes the existence of gender-neutral criteria of healthy systems. One alternative to the current practice of evaluating women by male-defined criteria is to develop gender-specific standards of adaptive interpersonal processes. Although this permits a more neutral assessment of individuals in families, it does not easily translate into description of the family system as a whole. Furthermore, it sets up gender-based dichotomies: the idealization of differentiation and the glorification of interconnection each oversimplify the complex conflicting needs of individuals in family systems.

Ultimately family therapists must develop criteria of highly functional or well-adapted family systems that encompass and synthesize prototypical male and female interactional qualities. But even if such abstract criteria are created and defined in gender-sensitive terms, family therapists cannot forget that they are applied to gendered human beings. Men and women do not reach "interdependency" by identical paths, nor is it as simple as helping a mother dilute her relationship with her children while inviting father to participate more in family life. A mother cannot simply separate if she lacks economic resources to do so, if she feels she has failed to fulfill her socially defined role, if the family resists her withdrawal from caretaking activities, or if she experiences a deep sense of loss or isolation when she is deprived of relational experiences crucial to her identity. A father cannot simply engage with his family when the public domain is structured in ways precluding his flexible availability, when he is asked to partake in activities he considers feminine or worthless, or when, regardless of his willingness, his intrapsychic development and socialization limit his ability to monitor and emotionally respond to others. Thus, the application of gender-neutral criteria of healthy systems functioning requires expanding systems formulations to include description of how gender-specific individual developmental paths, family roles, and social location strongly constrain the degree to which individual family members and family systems as a whole can change.

## SUMMARY

At this stage of the critical examination of family therapy, a primary focus on women in families is crucial to render visible and to legitimate what is currently camouflaged or invalidated by our theories. But it is important not to pit male and female defined models against one another. Each reflects only one side of the coin and provides opportunities as well as liabilities. As men and women struggle to reconcile their different and often conflicting experiences of self and relationships, it is essential to remember that these differences do not arise full blown out of nature. Although certain preferred transactional styles with their respective strengths and weaknesses are empirically associated with each sex, these polarities emerge from the socially structured inequality of men and women, the culturally constituted ideology of gender, and the gender-specific developmental paths of individuals raised in the contemporary family form. In spite of these constraints, it is incumbent upon family therapists to begin developing models that blend and value both attachment and separation, productivity and nurturance, rationality and emotion — in order to help actualize the full personal potential of women and of men.

## REFERENCES

Bernal, G. & Ysern, E. (1986). Family therapy and ideology. *Journal of Marital and Family Therapy, 12*, 129-135.

Bograd, M. (1984). Family systems approaches to wife battering: A feminist critique. *American Journal of Orthopsychiatry, 54*, 558-568.

Bograd, M. (1986a). A feminist examination of family systems models of violence against women in the family. In M. Ault-Riché (Ed.), *Women and family therapy*. Rockville, MD: Aspen Systems Corporation.

Bograd, M. (1986b). A feminist examination of family therapy: What is women's place? *Women and Therapy*, forthcoming.

Bograd, M. (1986c). Feminist perspectives on family systems theory: Power, gender and the family. In M. Douglas & L. Walker (Eds.), *Feminist psychotherapies: Integration of therapeutic and feminist systems*. New York: Ablex Publishing, forthcoming.

Bowen, M. (1971). The use of family theory in clinical practice. In J. Haley (Ed.), *Changing families: A family therapy reader*. New York: Grune & Stratton.

Bowen, M. (1978). *Family therapy in clinical practice*. New York: Jason Aronson.

Broverman, I., Broverman, D., Clarkson, F., Rosenkrantz, P. & Vogel, S. (1970). Sex-role stereotypes and clinical judgments of mental health. *Journal of Consulting and Clinical Psychology, 23*, 1-7.

Chodorow, N. (1978). *The reproduction of mothering: Psychoanalysis and the sociology of gender*. Berkeley: University of California Press.

Dinnerstein, D. (1976). *The mermaid and the minotaur: Sexual arrangements and human malaise*. New York: Harper & Row.

Eichenbaum, L. & Orbach, S. (1983). *What do women want: Exploding the myth of dependency*. New York: Coward-McCann.

Gilligan, C. (1982). *In a different voice: Psychological theory and women's development*. Cambridge, MA: Harvard University Press.

Goldner, V. (1985a). Feminism and family therapy. *Family Progress, 24*, 31-47.

Goldner, V. (1985b). The feminist critique: Its influence on the future of family therapy. Keynote presented at Harvard Medical School Continuing Education Department conference, "What Works in Family Therapy?," Cambridge, MA.

Goldner, V. (1985c). Warning: Family therapy may be hazardous to your health. *Family Therapy Networker, 9*, 18-23.

Hare-Mustin, R. (1978). A feminist approach to family therapy. *Family Process, 17*, 181-194.

Hare-Mustin, R. (1980). Family therapy may be dangerous for your health. *Professional Psychology, 11*, 935-938.

Jacobson, N. (1983). Beyond empiricism: The politics of marital therapy. *American Journal of Family Therapy, 11*, 11-24.

James, K. (1985). Breaking the chains of gender: Family therapy's position? *Australian Journal of Family Therapy, 5*, 241-248.

James, K. & McIntyre, D. (1983). The reproduction of families: The social role of family therapy? *Journal of Marital and Family Therapy, 9*, 119-129.

Jordan, J. (1983). Empathy and the mother-daughter relationship. *Work in Progress, No. 82-02*. Wellesley, MA: Stone Center Working Papers Series.

Joslyn, B. (1982). Shifting sex roles: The silence of the family therapy literature. *Clinical Social Work Journal, 10*, 39-51.

Layton, M. (1984). Tipping the therapeutic scales — Masculine, feminine, or neuter? *Family Therapy Networker, 8*, 20-27.

Lerner, H. (1983). Female dependency in context: Some theoretical and technical considerations. *American Journal of Orthopsychiatry, 53*, 697-705.

Luepnitz, D. (1984). Cybernetic baroque: The hi-tech talk of family therapy. *Family Therapy Networker, 8*, 37-41.

Margolin, G., Fernandes, V., Talovic, S. & Onorato, R. (1983). Sex role considerations and behavioral marital therapy: Equal does not mean identical. *Journal of Marital and Family Therapy, 9*, 131-145.

Miller, J. (1976). *Toward a new psychology of women*. Boston: Beacon Press.

Miller, J. (1984). The development of women's sense of self. *Work in Progress*. Wellesley, MA: Stone Center Working Papers Series.

Minuchin, S. (1974). *Families and family therapy*. Cambridge, MA: Harvard University Press.

Minuchin, S. & Fishman, C. (1981). *Family therapy techniques*. Cambridge, MA: Harvard University Press.

Rubin, L. (1983). *Intimate strangers: Men and women together*. New York: Harper & Row.

Schaef, A. (1981). *Women's reality: An emerging female system in the white male society*. Minneapolis: Winston Press.

Spender, D. (1980). *Man made language*. Boston: Routledge & Kegan Paul.

Stiver, I. (1984). The meanings of "dependency" in female-male relationships. *Work in Progress, No. 83-07*. Wellesley: Stone Center Working Papers Series.

Surrey, J. (1983). The relational self in women: Clinical implications. *Work in Progress, No. 82-02*. Wellesley, MA: Stone Center Working papers Series.

Surrey, J. (1984). The self-in-relation: A theory of women's development. *Work in Progress, No. 84-02*. Wellesley: Stone Center Working Papers Series.

Taggart, M. (1985). The feminist critique in epistemological perspective: Questions of context in family therapy. *Journal of Marital and Family Therapy, 11*, 113-126.

Women's Project in Family Therapy. (1982). Mothers and daughters. *Monograph Series, 1*.

Women's Project in Family Therapy. (1983). Mothers and sons, fathers and daughters. *Monograph Series, 2*.

## CLINICAL APPLICATIONS

# Women and Abuse in the Context of the Family

Margaret Cotroneo

**SUMMARY.** This article examines spouse/partner abuse from the vantage point of women and family therapy. The author's observations are drawn from over 10 years of systematic application of family and relational theory to the treatment of family violence. Issues and concepts about women and abuse are identified. The concept of parentification is used to organize and translate theory into implications for practice.

Powerful social, political, religious, economic, and psychological forces in our culture mitigate against a full exploration of the relational reality of the family. One of the avenues of exploration opened to us during the last 15 years has been intrafamilial violence.

Looking at families through the mirror of abuse has enabled us to examine our society's bias in favor of the preservation of the ideal or "normal" family (Thorne, 1982). This norm is largely rooted in a system of gender hierarchy that is retained by impeding woman's development and rendering her vantage point invisible in social in-

Margaret Cotroneo, RN, PhD, is Assistant Professor and Program Director, Psychiatric-Mental Health Nursing, School of Nursing, University of Pennsylvania, Philadelphia, PA.

teraction. Its conditions are cast in moral terms: being "normal" means being "good" or "perfect." Its retention has resulted in a dangerous denial of the imperfections, injustices, and inequalities that exist in family relationships. So influential is the bias toward "normality" that persons who are victims of intrafamilial abuse are often scapegoated for calling attention to their plight.

As women have told their stories about abuse and exploitation in the family, they have begun to chip away at the privatization that isolated them in the family and its ecosystem. Destructive labels such as "masochistic" and "collusive" that have been used to define woman's mode of relating have been challenged. Studies of gender-related influences on human behavior have identified the stereotypes which have crippled their development as persons (Deaux, 1984). All states and the District of Columbia have enacted laws to protect battered women (Center for Women Policy Studies, 1984).

In spite of the gains that have been made, however, the mental health of women in the context of their significant relationships remains an area of great concern (American Psychological Association, 1985). As the findings of Straus, Gelles, and Steinmetz (1980) proposed, the American family has become our society's most violent institution. The field of family therapy is only beginning the struggle to conceptualize the reality of woman's experience of living in the family (Bograd, 1984).

In this paper, I will examine the vantage point of women in one aspect of intrafamilial abuse, that of spouse/partner abuse. The conceptual framework which shapes my clinical work is that of contextual family therapy (Boszormenyi-Nagy & Spark, 1973; Boszormenyi-Nagy & Krasner, 1986). Issues of loyalty, trust, and justice that emerge in family therapy are explored and translated into practice implications.

The abused women that I have treated have been referred in several ways. Some have come as a consequence of a spouse being mandated to therapy by the court; some have been referred for depression or anxiety disorders and abuse was then exposed in the course of the treatment; a few have been referred by the attorneys whom they consulted about separation or divorce. I believe that the first step toward therapeutic intervention in family violence takes place when society insists on legal accountability for abusive behavior. The failure to address the question of legal accountability in clear terms from the outset continues to privatize the abuse and contributes to the peripheralization and overburdening of its victims (Cotroneo, 1986). For that reason, intervention in intrafamilial abuse requires a treatment plan that is developed through a process of interdisciplinary collaboration.

## WOMEN SPOUSE/PARTNER ABUSE: CONCEPTS AND ISSUES

Research in the area of spouse/partner abuse of women generally covers three areas: patterns of abuse and the reasons for their maintenance, theoretical constructs which explain behaviors, and clinical applications. Attempts to generalize are limited by sampling techniques and methodology. Most of what we know is based on self-volunteered samples. The study of clinical applications using a family systems conceptual framework is largely neglected (Bograd, 1984).

Conceptualizations of woman's experience in spouse abuse tend to develop around explanations for why women stay in relationships in which they are abused and otherwise exploited. These explanations are derived from a number of different perspectives: psychodynamic, social learning, developmental, biopsychosocial, and relational.

In a summary of the research on abused wives, Hilberman (1980) identifies a specific stress syndrome that is a consequence of violent abuse. Cast as a uniform psychological response, this syndrome is characterized by everpresent anxiety and fear of the unexpected, chronic apprehension of imminent doom, vigilance, overwhelming passivity and inability to act, a view of themselves as incompetent and unworthy, guilt and denial of anger, concern about loss of control, and feelings of powerlessness to make changes. Related findings are reported by Weingourt (1985) out of her experience with therapy groups for abused women. She identifies recurrent themes of loneliness, isolation, and fear of abandonment. She suggests that the fear of being alone results in the tendency to fuse with a stronger person who then does the living for both.

One of the most comprehensive studies of battered women was conducted by Walker (1980). Using a feminist analysis, she posited two important concepts about the behavior of women in abusive situations: the theory of learned helplessness and the cycle theory of violence. Learned helplessness in a social learning theory which proposes that women who are repeatedly exposed to abuse learn that no response will be effective in controlling violence. They come to believe that they have no influence on the success or failure of events that concern them. Consequently, their options for acting are restricted by their feelings of helplessness. The cycle theory of violence identifies three periods in the pattern of behavior: a tension building period, an acute battering incident, and a tension reduction period. The latter is characterized by kindness and contrite, loving behavior. Walker concludes from her findings that only when there is true equality between the sexes will there be a society free of violence.

In an early study which focused on abused wives and why they stay, Gelles (1976) interviewed members of 41 families (33 wives) in which the wife had been abused by her husband. He identified three factors which increased the likelihood that an abused wife would remain with the abuser: (1) if the episodes of violence were less frequent and less severe; (2) if the wife had a history of frequent physical abuse by her parents; and (3) if the wife had little power and few resources available to her. Of these three factors, a woman was least likely to leave an abusive marital situation if she had a history of severe physical abuse by her parents.

It is not clear from the literature in what ways a history of physical abuse in the family of origin affects a woman's help-seeking behaviors. In a study comparing 46 physically abused and 12 not physically abused women who sought refuge at a shelter, Star (1978) found that most of the physically abused women (65%) neither experienced nor witnessed physical abuse in their families. When she looked at the abusing husbands, however, she found that they more often came from families in which they experienced or witnessed physical abuse.

Labell (1979) studied 512 physically abused women who sought services from a shelter for battered women. Demographic data, previous history of violence, and contributing factors were examined for the women and their mates. She finds only minimal support for the theory that exposure to violence in childhood leads to greater acceptance of violence in adult life. Most of the women she interviewed (72%) had a history of reaching out to others for help but were unsuccessful in their attempts to change their situations. Labell also found that the incidence of a previous history of violence was higher for the males who were physically abusive. This latter finding is corroborated in Stahly's (1978) review of the literature of spousal violence and in a later study of abused wives and abusive husbands conducted by Rosenbaum and O'Leary (1981). Generally speaking, the connection between abused wives and violent families is not as strong as the connection between abusive husbands and violent families.

A survey by Goldberg and Tomlanovich (1984) of 275 females and 217 males who identified themselves as victims of domestic violence in the course of seeking treatment in a hospital emergency department found that most had difficulty believing their situation serious enough to seek help specific to the abuse. Instead, a current medical problem, a complaint of unexplained pain, an injury, the fact that one's children had been hurt, and a negative view of the overall relationship were identified as primary motivators for seeking help. Of the overall sample, battered women tended to view their relationships more negatively and to request counseling services more often.

Even when battered women seek help initially, they may not persist. Minimal material resources and the lack of institutional and social support are major factors. The emergence of battered women's shelters may eventually yield some better data. Sheltering strikes at the heart of isolation by suddenly immersing a woman in a communal living situation that minimizes the gap between her experience and that of other women, helping her feel secure and protected (Bowker & Maurer, 1985). Sheltering may also help women to build a social support network of their own. Mitchell and Hodson (1983) suggest that the more a woman's social ties overlap with those of her partner, the more difficult it may be for her to obtain support in dealing with the battering situation. In addition, increased levels of violence are associated with a greater likelihood that the responses of friends may be characterized by avoidance and discomfort. Thus, even friendships may be unavailable as supportive resources for moving out of an abusive relationship.

The data available on help-seeking behavior of abused women tends to be collected from wives who seek help and is merely demographic. We know very little about how women's experiences in their family of origin affect their needs, wants, concerns, and expectations in subsequent relationships. An exploration of the modes of relating in a woman's family of origin may yield more helpful information about both treatment and prevention of spouse/partner abuse.

## VICTIMS, VICTIMIZERS, AND RELATIONSHIPS

The need to mobilize concern for women in situations of abuse has resulted in the tendency to generalize their experience under the category "victim." This focus has served to mobilize social concern, establish social responsibility for intervention, and hold perpetrators accountable for abuse. However, it is not clear that the victim stance empowers women themselves. When women are defined as victims, their entitlement to consideration is contingent upon the responsiveness of others. This reinforces their inclination to adapt their choices to the expectations of people upon whom they depend while their own wants, needs, and contributions are taken for granted. Furthermore, it feeds a cycle of self-doubt as women may come to believe that whatever happens to them, happens simply because they are women.

One of the major disadvantages of continuing to focus on the victim aspect of woman's experience in family violence is the emphasis this places on the pathology of their relationships. Often women get preoccupied in finding a reason why they seem to find hurting rather than caring partners. They conclude there must be something wrong with them because they continue to allow themselves to be "used."

Defining a relationship in victim-victimizer terms tends to prescribe rather than elicit what is going on between people. It tends to work from the presumption that victims and victimizers are in opposition to each other and ignores the dialectic process that shapes all relationships over time. Clinical work with families demonstrates that the hand that hurts is also the one that heals in the sense that confronting rather than avoiding the source of injury builds self-trust rather than self-doubt. A one-dimensional consideration of family relationships cannot account for the whole of the abuse situation no matter how much it may serve to correct an injustice. This is especially relevant in situations in which women choose to remain with their abusers. In these situations, removing the abuser from the realm of therapeutic concern only functions to increase the abused person's guilt and blame. Consequently, women are often diverted from their major agenda of establishing equity in close relationships and are trapped into making impossible choices between commitment and freedom as if these two were invariably in opposition. When this happens, options and resources for healing relationships are ignored or denied.

In my observations of abused women in family therapy, I find that it is not relationships that exploit. Rather, it is modes of relating that shape a process of exploitation over time. A large part of the therapeutic work centers on building trust in the self as a person who can take responsibility for her/his own well-being in the context of caring about others and being responsive to their needs and expectations.

Among the most promising contributions to conceptualizing woman's mode of relating are those of Carol Gilligan and her colleagues (Gilligan, 1982; Lyons, 1983). Their work crosses disciplinary boundaries and gives impetus to the call for new ways of conceptualizing relationships between women and men. Out of her studies of moral development, Gilligan (1982) proposed two distinct forms of self-definition in relation to others. They are separation and connection. Separation is characterized by independence, self-sufficiency, and autonomy while connection is characterized by interdependence, mutual reliance, and responsibility for others. Separation is oriented toward an ethic of justice and rights. Relationship is experienced as reciprocity between separate individuals who are rooted in roles and operate out of rules of fairness. A basic rule is to consider others as one would like to be considered (Lyons, 1983). The mode of connection is oriented toward an ethic of care and response. Relationship is experienced as response to others on their terms, with a concern for their well-being and the alleviation of their burdens. Gilligan proposes that men more typically construct their relationships in terms of separation and women in terms of connection (Gilligan, 1982). She does not view the different orientations of women and men as biologically determined but rather that they derive out of childhood experiences of inequality and interdependence. With equal frequency, both women and men construct a self definition that is organized in terms of relationship to others (Lyons, 1983). Sensitivity to the needs and expectations of others can be identified in both spouses/partners when couples are treated conjointly. The following case vignette may serve to illustrate this point:

Sam was court ordered to therapy for a single incident of physical abuse. The entire marriage had been characterized by psychological abuse in the form of control of Sarah's movements, child rearing behaviors, and the family's financial resources. It was also marked by verbal denigration and inappropriate sexual demands. This was a long-term marriage with seven children. In these cases, I usually see the abuser alone on a bi-monthly basis and the couple together every 6 weeks.

Both assumed a position of entitlement to exclusive consideration. Both felt that they had put their own needs aside because they felt intimidated by the anticipated response of the other. Sarah felt she could not say what she thought because she generally received a critical, hostile response. From his side, Sam said he never spoke up to ask for what he wanted because whatever he said would not be "right" in Sarah's eyes. Sam used his anger to make his claims and get his own way.

Sarah used placating behaviors to try to achieve the same end. Neither felt s(he) had ever had any real power to influence the other. Each felt the other got her/his own way all of the time. The therapeutic work emphasized helping each partner to develop a trustworthy self in relation to the other.

A consideration of gender-related modes of relating and power inequities are necessary in working with spouse/partner abuse. The failure to do so sets the stage for repeating the inequities of the past with all their destructive consequences.

These concepts are often difficult to integrate within a family systems framework. Family therapy has traditionally been framed in egalitarian terms. The family therapist tries to remain open to the needs and concerns of all family members while at the same time being partial to the rights and welfare of the person who has been abused. This has sometimes been viewed as being "soft" on abuse by people outside the field. Yet, it seems to me that the task of family therapists who treat intrafamilial abuse is to continue to care about what families care about; that is, to care about the whole unit of relationship and to care about each individual in her or his particular struggle. New concepts to integrate these concerns can be shaped out of this fundamental respect for the experience of the people who are most affected by the abuse.

## IMPLICATIONS FOR PRACTICE

Taking care of one's own well-being and caring about the well-being of others is integral to the mental health of every person. In situations of intrafamilial abuse, caring is distorted and exploited.

Those who intervene are often confused and frustrated by the elements of caring that persist even in the face of pervasive mistrust. There are numerous examples of abused women who continue to respond to their abusers with care, consideration, and protection. Many women clients have reported that they would leave the abusive relationship except they do not believe their spouses/partners could make it alone. They are preoccupied with doing the "right" thing; that is, taking action that is least likely to hurt their abuser. Such responses contradict reason and reality, however, they reflect a genuine conflict about what is owed to self vs. what is owed to others that can be paralyzing. Loyalty of this nature characterizes abusive families. It is shaped by expectations of care and devotion held in common among family members and transmitted from generation to generation. Loyalty is like an invisible intergenerational tapestry woven from the fibers of caring relationships (Boszormenyi-Nagy & Spark, 1973). Although it often goes unacknowledged in the family, it is considered to be a powerful motivator of behavior.

The dynamics of loyalty can be identified, not only in spouse/partner abuse, but in all kinds of intrafamilial abuse. The mother-daughter relationship in the father-daughter incest configuration is another example of family loyalty at work. It is generally assumed that the mother has abdicated parenting and spouse/partner activities to her daughter. Treatment is often directed toward helping her to execute her role as daughter's advocate and helping her take back the activities she has abdicated. However, a strong bond often exists between mother and daughter that is both benefit and burden for each of them and keeps them emotionally linked to each other. What is often not adequately explored in treatment is the entitlement position of the mother, i.e., how benefits, burdens, and power are distributed in her own life. Such an exploration would include a consideration of her relationship to her family of origin. An exploration of the entitlement position of the mother might be a more beneficial context for exploring the daughter's painful issue of the mother's failure to protect her against exploitation and the mother's denial of the responsibility to protect that is implicit in caring for a dependent child.

Loyalty and the shame that accompanies loyal behaviors toward an abuser are among the most difficult aspects of intrafamilial abuse for clients to explore. Therefore they can easily be ignored under the pressure of crisis intervention that characterizes much of the treatment of these families. Responsibility is prescribed, rather than being elicited in the context of a dialogue among all those who have been affected by what has happened. Many women who have been exploited as children report that they have never had an opportunity for face-to-face exploration within the family about what happened and how they have been affected. Yet, it is how the important people in their lives responded to them around the issues of abandonment, betrayal of trust, conflicting loyalties, and entitlement to justice that shapes the lifelong pain of women in abusive situations. When accountability is not elicited in a dialogue among all those who are affected by the abuse, the abused client is left to carry the burden of guilt and shame for the whole family. In spite of what abused women themselves report about the consequences of abuse, family therapy is not the treatment of choice at the point of entry into abusive families. More often than not, its methods and concepts are considered ineffective when the goal is to separate the abused and the abuser. It is introduced only later, when it is clear that the family means to stay together and this may be the least effective point of entry. While there can be no compromise on the position that violence against another, whether physical or psychological, is unacceptable, there remains a further obligation to raise questions about whether interventions that are applied are a faithful expression of what is beneficial to people in the places where they actually struggle. In my experience with intrafamilial abuse, family therapy is most helpful when it is applied as a treatment of choice.

In my work I use the relational concept of parentification (Boszormenyi-Nagy & Spark, 1973) to explain the mode of relating associated with loyalty. Parentification is characterized by inappropriate expectations for care and devotion that are enslaving. Persons who are parentified carry a burden of guilt-laden obligation for the well-being of others while their own needs go unacknowledged. The parentified one is bound to the relationship through a process of giving and receiving which is counterautonomous. Because she does not feel entitled to speak on her own terms, she makes her choices contingent upon the expectations of others.

A person becomes sensitized to parentification in the family of origin. When parents, for whatever reason and regardless of fault, cannot appropriately give to their children, the children tend to react to the loss of care with greater emotional attachment. They become parents to their parents in order to get parenting. Whatever gains they receive are received by meeting the parents' needs. Asking for something for oneself is associated with selfishness. Because all children are deeply committed to a continuing relationship to their parents, they take on parental burdens and failures as their own, often reacting with emotions of shame, guilt, and resentment. Thus emotionally bound, they are not free to give appropriately in relationships outside the family unless and until they come to terms with the loss or deprivation of care they have experienced in the family of origin. In the context of parentification, staying in an abusive relationship may be a protective action or affirmation of loyalty to the code of fairness shaped in the family of origin. In intrafamilial abuse, this code of fairness requires that care for others must take precedence over care for the self.

Parentification is an intensely painful experience for women primarily because their contributions go unacknowledged. As one of my female clients put it: "It would help a lot if someone would just say to me that they know how hard it is. It's like I get blamed for being tired." Another woman reported: "I grew up believing I didn't have any rights." Resentment is shaped by the lack of acknowledgment and becomes paralyzing.

Sometimes in our zeal to protect our clients from further abuse, we forget about the pain of parentification. Women are frequently blamed for what seems to be passivity and adaptation in the face of abuse. In being strong for others, they appear to be weak. By protecting their partners, they become sponges for failure and perceive themselves as incompetent. Failing to please their partner, they no longer trust their own judgment. Their thinking reflects their experience, as they continue to assign to themselves the responsibility for their partner's problems, hurts, and failures.

The following is one woman's description of her experience of parentification in a case of long-term spouse abuse:

> You have just gone off to work and my knees are still shaking. I know that you couldn't possibly understand. It seems that I wake up with a feeling of doom and what did I do today and what am I going to be lectured about today. You left and the dog was being terrific. He was standing at the door. He was wonderful. The minute you walked out the door, he grabbed my shoe again and there was a mad chase around the living room. I was doing exactly the same thing that you did however it just doesn't come out the same. I feel the same total lack of respect from the dog that I do from you and I guess the children sometimes, like I am really not here.

In working with women clients who are abused, I work toward de-parentification. The therapeutic work is guided by three major considerations: (1) acknowledging the contributions that have previously been taken for granted; (2) exploration and discouragement of the means of parentification; and (3) a retracing of the path of parentification that occurred in the family of origin.

## Acknowledgment

Acknowledgment is more than a simple tool for communication. It arises out of one's vision, concern, and appreciation of the client's reality. The first priority in working with abused women is to elicit the story of their experience on their own terms. The therapist needs to remain open to the client's perspective on what she has given and what she has gained in the relationship. Questions which seek to elicit her contributions not only to the spouse/partner relationship but to all her relationships help her to take more responsibility for her own well-being and elicit her sense of being unjustly treated. The acknowledgment of unfairness by the therapist begins to open up a larger context for examining the abuse. This should be done without blame or scapegoating of the abuser on the part of the therapist. Otherwise, the client can be caught in a loyalty conflict and might be forced to reaffirm her loyalty to the spouse/partner by distancing herself from the therapy. The message of the therapist that would be most helpful is a solid, straightforward advocacy of the female client that, at the same time, allows for the humanization and personalization of her abuser. To genuinely advocate for an abused woman is to extend due consideration to all those relationships that are important to her, with their resources as well as their limitations. It is a way of extending trust to women who have grown accustomed to being criticized for caring.

Early in the therapy, it is also important to begin to nurture any small act on the part of the client to take more control of her situation. What makes sense to her in terms of protecting herself? What does she want to do immediately? The emphasis is on helping the client learn to trust her own judgment and define her own terms. As long as she is willing to make her own safety and that of her children an immediate priority, the client should be supported into designing her own strategy for guaranteeing safety.

The therapists who work with abused women have a responsibility to make themselves and to make their clients aware of the legal and social resources that can be made available to the client and also how they ordinarily work for and against clients. Sheltering is one of the most significant of these resources (Bowker & Maurer, 1985).

Encouraging the client to tell her story to others, including parents and siblings, is also necessary in order to intervene early in the feelings of shame and guilt and thereby to allow the resentment to surface. Clinicians are sometimes reluctant to encourage an abused woman to talk to members of her family of origin because their initial response may be inappropriately intrusive or even blaming. However, it has been my experience that confronting this loyalty system directly is ultimately strengthening because it has the effect of reducing fear and dysfunctional protective behaviors within the abusive relationship.

### Discouraging the Means of Parentification

Unless she chooses otherwise, I generally see an abused woman alone in the first session. I see a great deal of benefit, however, in seeing her together with a person(s) she designates as supportive. As soon as possible, the client and the abuser should be seen together with the children. The abuse should be discussed conjointly and its reality confronted. Every attempt to minimize or avoid what happened should be challenged by the therapist. The incident that precipitated the help-seeking behavior should be discussed in detail with consideration of what effects the discussion might have on the children. The therapist has a responsibility to give a clear message that force and coercion are unacceptable modes of relating in the family and cannot be justified on any basis. What is acceptable, however, is for each family member to say how they have been affected by what has occurred and to expect the consideration they need and want. The "I" statement is one of the first steps in deparentification. The therapist is in the position of helping the family members become more expert in identifying their modes of relating and the elements that are constructive as well as those that are destructive.

I also see the abuser and the children separately. This serves to address some of the fusion among family members by hearing each one's side on her/his own terms. In working with children, I want to know how they have been affected. I elicit their concern for themselves, their parents, and their siblings. It is important to ask children how they have tried to be helpful to their parent(s) and to bring to the surface conflicts of loyalty. It is important to work with them to relieve them from the burden of responsibility that children carry in intrafamilial abuse. The therapist needs to ask about physical and sexual abuse of children that is often present in cases of spouse/ partner abuse. Depression in these children is often masked. Questions about suicide should be asked. Very young children often feel responsible for keeping the family together. Older children often have difficulty dealing constructively with anger. They tend to fear loss of relationships that they need and want.

In working with abusers it is important to focus on controlling the destructive behaviors by emphasizing two dimensions: (1) taking responsibility for the abuse; and (2) their expectations of themselves in the family and in the workplace. Whatever social-legal controls that are necessary to intervene in the abusive behavior should be employed. The point cannot be made strongly enough that therapy without social-legal controls merely supports the privatization of abuse in our society. It is often very difficult for clinicians themselves to move abuse from the privacy of the therapy room to the social-legal forum. This is particularly true of spouse abuse. In the face of the evidence available to us about the consequences of privatization of abuse, the failure to move its consideration into the social-legal forum goes beyond sheer paternalism. It calls into question the competence of the therapist to work with abusive families.

Controlling the abusive behavior is one aspect of working with the abuser; the other is to elicit their perspective on the burdens and benefits they experienced in their significant relationships. Abusers tend to take a position of extreme entitlement to unilateral consideration. However, their genuine entitlement to ask for what they need has been consistently diminished by exploitative actions. Therefore, they use force to strengthen their claim to entitlement. Talking about the abusers' sense of being overburdened is an essential avenue to helping them take more responsibility for their own actions. This is not an attempt to exonerate the abuser but rather an attempt to humanize their side of things.

### *Retracing the Path of Parentification*

Violence in the family is so crisis-oriented that family of origin work often seems extraneous. In my experience with intrafamilial abuse, both short-term and long-term changes in modes of relating require confrontation with the resources and limitations of the family of origin. I direct both the abused client and the abuser back to their families of origin to open a discussion of what has been going on in the nuclear family. When parents are still living, this kind of talking can take place directly and it is a very positive therapeutic signal. Grandparents and other family members are asked to come to one or more sessions to discuss the dimensions of parentification. Even when parents are dead or unavailable, other methods of facing family of origin issues need to be attempted.

Family of origin work reverses the parentification in the relationship to one's own parents because it intervenes in the tendency to protect one's parents from one's own needs and wants. The reversal of parentification comes in the claim to receive care and consideration as opposed to the obligation to extend care. This sets the stage for reconnecting to the family of origin on a more appropriate level. In my experience, genuine attempts to reopen the relationship to the family of origin on a new basis can be freeing, regardless of the outcome.

## CONCLUSION

One of the most important aspects of family therapy with abused women is creating a climate of trust in which they are free to speak on their own terms and free to claim their entitlement to equity of care and consideration. This is best done by advocating for them within, not outside, the context of their significant relationships. De-parentification is one aspect of this process. It is oriented toward helping women shape a trust-based definition of self in relation to others.

## REFERENCES

American Psychological Association (1985). *A women's mental health agenda*. Washington, DC: Author.

Bograd, Michele (1984). Family systems approaches to wife battering: A feminist critique. *American Journal of Orthopsychiatry, 54*, 558-568.

Boszormenyi-Nagy, I., & Krasner, B. (1986). *Between give and take: A clinical guide to contextual therapy*. New York; Brunner/Mazel.

Boszormenyi-Nagy, I. & Spark, G. (1973). *Invisible loyalties: Reciprocity in intergenerational family relationships*. New York: Harper and Row.

Bowker, L. & Maurer, L. (1985). The importance of sheltering in the lives of battered women. *Response, 8*, 2-8.

Center for Women Policy Studies (1984). Wife abuse: The facts. *Response, 7*, 9-10.

Cotroneo, M. (1986). Families and abuse. In *Family Resources*, M. Karpel (Ed.), New York: Brunner/Mazel.

Deaux, K. (1984). From individual differences to social categories. Analysis of a decade's research on gender. *American Psychologist, 39*, 105-16.

Gelles, R. (1976). Abused wives: Why do they stay. *Journal of Marriage and the Family, 38*, 659-668.

Gilligan, C. (1982). *In a different voice: Psychological theory and women's development.* Cambridge, MA: Harvard University Press.

Goldberg, W. & Tomlanovich, M. (1984). Domestic violence victims in the emergency department: New findings. *Journal of the American Medical Association, 251*, 3259-3264.

Hilberman, E. (1980). Overview: The "wife-beater's wife" reconsidered. *American Journal of Psychiatry, 137*, 1336-1347.

Labell, L. (1979). Wife abuse: A sociological study of battered women and their mates. *Victimology: An International Journal, 4*, 258-267.

Lyons, N. (1983). Two perspectives: On self, relationships, and morality. *Harvard Educational Review, 53*, 125-145.

Mitchell, R. & Hodson, C. (1983). Coping with domestic violence: Social support and psychological health among battered women. *American Journal of Community Psychology, 11*, 629-654.

Rosenbaum, A. & O'Leary, K. (1981). Marital violence: Characteristics of abusive couples. *Journal of Consulting and Clinical Psychology, 49*, 63-71.

Stahly, G. (1978). A review of select literature of spousal violence. *Victimology, 2*, 591-607.

Star, B. (1978). Comparing battered and non-battered women. *Victimology: An International Journal, 3*, 32-44.

Straus, M., Gelles, R. & Steinmetz, S. (1980). *Behind closed doors: Violence in the American family.* New York: Anchor Press.

Thorne, B. (1982). Feminist rethinking of the family: An overview. In Thorne (Ed.), *Rethinking the Family: Some Feminist Questions.* New York: Longman.

Walker, L. (1979). *The battered woman.* New York: Harper Colophon Books.

Weingourt, R. (1985). Never to be alone: Existential therapy with battered women. *Journal of Psychosocial Nursing and Mental Health Services, 23*, 24-30.

# Female Legacies:
# Intergenerational Themes
# and Their Treatment for Women
# in Alcoholic Families

### Claudia Bepko

**SUMMARY.** Alcoholism poses special dilemmas for women. This paper reviews some of the gender-linked effects of alcoholic behavior in families by tracing the experiences of the women in one alcoholic family through three generations. The case study focuses specifically on patterns of over- and underresponsible functioning in these women as the dominant clinical issue and outlines the ways in which a Bowen systems approach can effectively reverse dysfunctional patterns.

Research exploring intergenerational and developmental antecedents of alcoholism for both men and women is very limited, but is a growing focus of attention (Gomberg & Lisansky, 1984). While some studies attempt to establish a genetic basis for transmission of alcoholism through successive generations in families (Goodwin, 1976, 1979; Bohman et al., 1981), others focus on issues of developmental disruption and parental drinking as possible predictors of recurrent alcoholism from one generation to another (Cotton, 1979; Gomberg, 1980).

Research exploring these issues for women alcoholics sheds very little light on the emotional and behavioral dynamics in families that may result in alcohol abuse (Wilsnack, 1982). Further, even less is known about the dynamics that result in involvement with an alcoholic spouse, or in the outcome that a woman is the mother of an alcoholic child. Neither does research comment in more than a descriptive way on the fact that women suffer the more serious consequences of alcoholism in the family in the form of rape, incest,

---

Claudia Bepko, MSW, is the Co-Director of Family Therapy Associates, 718 River Road, Fair Haven, NJ 07701. She is the author, with Jo-Ann Krestan, of *The Responsibility Trap: A Blueprint for Treating The Alcoholic Family* published by Free Press in 1984.

physical abuse, higher rates of depression, and in operating in the generally more stigmatized role assigned to a female versus a male drinker.

The purpose of this discussion is to propose a paradigm for viewing the experience of the woman in the alcoholic family, to track the evolution of that experience through three generations exploring the similarities and differences between the drinking and nondrinking women in a given family, and to outline an approach to treatment based on Bowen family systems theory.

## ALCOHOLIC SYSTEMS: SPECIAL ISSUES FOR WOMEN

Recent work exploring the alcoholic family as a whole from a systemic perspective has focused on the adaptive nature of roles that evolve as the family organizes around drinking behavior. Those who relate to the drinker, particularly those in the immediate family system, develop behaviors that are adaptive to changes occurring in the drinker (Davis, Berenson, Steinglass & Davis, 1974) so that a circular form of interaction is established in which the family reacts to the alcoholism and the drinker reacts to the family reacting. Over time, the entire system becomes characterized by oscillating extremes of in control/out of control, or of what Berenson (1976) refers to as "wet" and "dry" behavior. A very serious distortion of the feelings and needs of family members creates an emotional environment in which distrust, fear, and lowered self-esteem are dominant landmarks. Family interactions become either chaotic or rigid, the family closes off and isolates itself from the extended family and its larger social sphere, and family members assume roles that are geared toward survival (Black, 1981), reduction of anxiety (Jackson, 1954), attempts to bolster self-esteem, and an often "compulsive" need to create order in what is experienced as a very disordered environment. Because the people who relate to the alcoholic acquire very dysfunctional roles and a very distorted sense of their own identity, they are highly prone to develop compulsive or addictive problems themselves.

As the recent growing feminist critique in family therapy has noted, however, families in general and alcoholic families in particular have not, with the exception of Bepko and Krestan (1985), been studied with an understanding of the way that gender differences influence the type of adaptive roles that individuals assume. Nor has gender been considered a significant factor in the larger social context in which addictive problems in families emerge. General research has, however, indicated some major distinctions between males and females who drink.

Women alcoholics are more isolated than men; their drinking is more stigmatized (Beckman, 1975; Sandmaier, 1980); and they suffer generally from greater guilt, shame, and low self-esteem (Corrigan, 1980; Babcock-Connor, 1981; Beckman, 1978). They are more likely than men to abuse prescription drugs (Gomberg, 1976; Morrissey, 1978). Their drinking problem develops or progresses more quickly than a male's (Curlee, 1970; Elder, 1973) and is more likely to be related to specific life cycle stresses or gynecological/endocrine problems (Curlee, 1970; Wilsnack, 1973). There is a high correlation for women between drinking and divorce (Johnson et al., 1977; Wilsnack, 1980).

Since it is rare that a woman who is alcoholic is not also either the daughter, wife, or mother of an alcoholic as well, to talk about women and alcoholism is to describe a continuum along which alcoholism and co-alcoholism cannot be viewed as distinct phenomenon, but rather as reciprocal or complementary responses to similar emotional processes.

Whether the woman drinks herself or is affected by another's drinking, certain common outcomes are predictable and they differ from the outcomes of male drinking. Drinking will reinforce a woman's already ascribed one-down status. Women who drink are viewed as sicker than men who drink, and women whose spouses or children drink are considered to be at fault. In general for all women, drinking intensifies a sense of shame, responsibility, and guilt. Alcoholism anywhere in a system intensifies the likelihood that women will experience abuses such as incest, rape, battering, eating disorders, marital/sexual problems, and depression, or will abuse themselves (Black, 1981; Greenblatt & Schuckit, 1976; Wilsnack & Beckman, 1984).

## OVERRESPONSIBILITY AND UNDERRESPONSIBILITY: A CLINICAL PARADIGM

The primary focus of this discussion is the difference between male and female roles in alcoholic systems that arise in the dimensions of over and underresponsibility. The concept of overfunctioning was first developed by Murray Bowen (1978) and it refers to the reciprocity that occurs in a dyadic relationship as two people regulate the amount of responsibility assumed by each for various functional and emotional aspects of the relationship. Bateson described a paradigm for a complementary relationship in terms of the equation A does more so B does less. Since women are culturally conditioned to be overresponsible for the emotional and physical well-being of others, they tend to fall more often than men into an overresponsible role.

If the male drinks, the wife assumes greater functional and emotional responsibility and thereby gains greater covert control. If the woman drinks, she is more stigmatized than the male because drinking undermines her capacity to function in her appointed role as wife and mother. She overtly disempowers herself though her symptoms powerfully dominate the system. If the woman herself drinks, alcohol may function to relieve the sense of perfectionism, rigidity, and pressure inherent in the overresponsible role because drinking permits a flip to underresponsible behavior. If the woman is the co-alcoholic (drinking by the male), alcohol may function to permit the power and control inherent in her increasing overresponsible behavior to emerge without forcing an acknowledgment of the meaning of her behavior. In either case, one function of alcohol is to make tolerable the constricting and paradoxical demands of the female role — on the one hand drinking relieves the pressure of being a caretaker and on the other it permits a forbidden sense of power. Ultimately it provides punishment for both.

These covert versus overt issues of power and dependency dominate the clinical picture — the addictive system becomes a mirror for the fundamental paradox of gender issues in families: men are socialized to show autonomy and hide dependence while women are socialized to show dependence and hide autonomy. Alcohol permits either suppression or expression of impulses that run counter to these contradictory constraints.

Patterns of over and underresponsibility ultimately have their origins in multigenerational patterns. The emotional and functional overfocus on others that is a characteristic of the female role results in a complementary underresponsibility for self. So that a wife, for instance, overfocused emotionally on a drinking husband neglects her own needs or communicates them indirectly to a child. The child, perhaps the oldest daughter, begins to overfocus on the mother emotionally and fails to differentiate any clear sense of her own needs. This daughter marries an alcoholic male, and the patterns are perpetuated. Other children in the family may assume various other complementary roles with regard to levels of over and underfunctioning in the family or in relationship to the other parent.

The daughter who becomes emotionally overfocused on her mother (or on her father in some different family configurations) may either sustain her patterns of overfunctioning into the next generation, or she may drink alcoholically (or develop some other compulsive or addictive behavior) in response to the failure to adequately focus on and differentiate her own needs from those of the emotional ego mass of the family. If the focus of her emotional overfunctioning is in turn her own daughter, this daughter is equally likely to develop an alcohol problem since the parental overfocus will elicit a complementary underresponsibility for self that will equally result in underdeveloped skills for coping with individual needs and impulses. Since these unbalanced interactions along the dimensions of over and underresponsibility take place in a context in which women are in fact socialized to be overly responsible for others and underresponsible for self, alcoholism has the effect of doubly oppressing women as they attempt to navigate the contradictions of their assigned roles. The subjective experience of either the drinking or the overfunctioning woman is frequently the same: low self-esteem, feelings of powerlessness, inadequacy, rage, fear, and a limited capacity for satisfying intimacy or closeness. In short, the woman reacts to the socially prescribed mandate to de-self by engaging in a process in which she further dilutes her sense of self either by drinking or by intensifying her overfocus on others.

## CASE STUDY

The following case describes the generational progression of alcoholism in one woman's family of origin and provides a framework for illustrating a course of treatment for an alcohol-affected woman.

Margaret is a 32-year-old woman who is the oldest daughter of three in her family of origin. Both Margaret's parents, Joe and Claire, are alcoholic. At the time Margaret enters treatment, Joe is actively drinking and Claire has stopped but refuses treatment. Joe is a youngest son and the only known alcoholic in his family of origin. Claire is an only child whose father was alcoholic. Margaret's next youngest sister is married to an alcoholic. The third and youngest sister appears to be in a stable marriage but suffers from chronic asthma and an eating disorder. There are no male siblings. Margaret has sought treatment because of her growing anxiety about her father's intensifying drinking. She is also recently divorced and in a new relationship with a recovering alcoholic. She frequently has outbursts of rage and is anxious about the unfamiliar patterns of interaction that occur in this relationship.

Since an awareness of the subjective experience of a woman in response to alcoholism is crucial to an understanding of how she plays out an adaptive response to it, the following descriptions discuss each woman in Margaret's family individually. The descriptions convey some of the affective sense or belief system of each woman as she describes herself and they outline the significant interactional dynamics involved among family members.

### Margaret's Grandmother

Margaret's grandmother (Claire's mother) was the spouse of an often violent, acting out, sometimes dysfunctional alcoholic. Her belief was that it was important to "stand by" him. She went to work, took on responsibility for much of the maintenance of the home, and provided most of the stability in the family. She infantilized and overfocused on Margaret's mother, Claire, in an attempt to compensate for her husband's abuse. The caretaking was primarily *functional*, however. The two did not share much emotional closeness because the mother's emotional focus was on the alcoholic.

In other words, she did too much for Claire but emotionally was able to give very little. She compensated for her own anger, neediness, and fear by overfocusing on the alcoholic and chronically felt guilty and somehow responsible for his drinking. Many times, she drank herself to keep him company. When he died, she felt tremendous guilt at her own sense of relief. Her anger and guilt were ultimately numbed by pain pills and tranquilizers. Outwardly she was a gentle, loving woman who almost never expressed anger. As she aged, she increasingly expected, though never directly asked for, care-taking from her daughter and granddaughters.

### Margaret's Mother

Claire was an only child who saw herself as almost completely dependent on her mother yet felt that she had been emotionally neglected and deprived by her. Claire's relationship with her father was characterized by fear, emotional abuse, neglect, absence of parenting, and continual moves necessitated by his inability to keep a job. As things became more insecure in the family, Claire's mother compensated by infantilizing Claire more. Claire consequently became somewhat phobic, very isolated, and depended almost entirely on her mother and eventually her own children to meet her physical and emotional needs. She became chronically negative, anxious, and conveyed the expectation that she "should" be taken care of by others.

Although she deeply wanted to be taken care of she married an alcoholic male who rarely was able to adequately meet this need. Claire somewhat repeated her mother's role—she became a perfectionistic caretaker who functioned well, at least within the sphere of domestic responsibility. Her alcoholic drinking progressed markedly at the time that Margaret left for college. Her drinking relieved the pressure of her overfunctioning and underscored her inability to focus effectively on her own needs and well-being. It also represented a reaction to Margaret's separating from the family.

Claire suffered from a deep sense of inadequacy and extreme social isolation. She married Joe because she felt he "understood" her. Yet, probably as a result of the emotional abuse and criticism she experienced with her father and the conflicting messages about dependency communicated by her mother, she remained emotionally detached from Joe. Their relationship was characterized by a covert mutual protectiveness. Both competed for the dependent role and when one drank the other would be sober. Their relationship was strained, tense, and hostile. Joe very vocally demanded to be treated like the "man" in the family and constantly told Claire she was an inadequate wife. Claire conveyed a clear message that she felt intellectually and socially superior to Joe and demanded material things that she knew he couldn't provide. In other words she married a man who could function as a scapegoat for her anger.

### Margaret's Sisters

Margaret's middle sister had an overly close relationship with Joe and would often state emphatically that he was the most important person in her life, more important ultimately than her husband or her young daughter. She felt she was the only one to truly understand Joe. As Joe's drinking progressed, this sister and her husband decided to have a child. Her secret hope was that it would be the male child that Joe had always wished for and that having a male grandchild would motivate him to stop drinking. With her husband she remained detached and focused most of her energy on her career. In an attempt not to repeat what she perceived as Claire's overdependence on her children, she remained at a fixed emotional distance from her young daughter as well.

Margaret's younger sister was closer to her mother, Claire, but clearly suffered from the emotional neglect characteristic of an alcoholic home. She became asthmatic, chronically sick, and had finally decided to marry the first and only man she had ever dated fearing that no other man would want her. It was clear that her husband would be her "caretaker." She planned to be a housewife and raise children.

### Margaret

Margaret assumed the position of the perfect parental child whose role it was to take care of her parents' needs for self-esteem and to referee some of the hostility and competitiveness between them. She became highly overresponsible, often taking on major roles in the maintenance of the house, maintenance of holiday rituals, as well as successfully maintaining an academic career including many extracurricular pursuits. The more she did, the more she was criticized by her parents for not doing more. She became hard on herself, emotionally constricted, perfectionistic, and during her entire adolescence never dated. Only when she left home and attended college did she begin to struggle with her lack of relationship skills and her lack of emotional development. She continued to have little sense of her own worth apart from what she could achieve and she continued to feel vaguely if not at times insistently responsible for her mother's happiness and well-being while feeling sure that she was unable to do anything about her own.

She is disturbed by her current relationship because it generates so much anger—it is her image of herself that she is loving, not an angry person. She therefore externalizes the source of her anger and places it on her lover—she defines the alcoholic as bad and as "causing" her anger. In this relationship she focuses almost all her emotional energy on her partner and is functionally overresponsible in almost all areas of the relationship.

### Family Patterns and Issues

As is true in many alcoholic families, a prime issue is the way that dependency needs are or are not dealt with. While all people are dependent, alcoholic families are characterized by dysfunctional adaptations to, expressions of, feelings of, and demands for caretaking or emotional responsiveness. These "adaptations" result in extremes of over and underresponsibility that help to maintain drinking as a potential correction for the pressures of being overresponsible versus the pain of being in the underresponsible or overtly dependent role.

The females in Margaret's family are all in some way prototypes of the typical adaptations women may make in what is or becomes an alcoholic environment.

Margaret's grandmother overfunctions both functionally and emotionally for her husband, overfunctions functionally for her daughter, and, unable to articulate or deal effectively with her own needs, she ultimately abuses drugs and maintains an overfunctioning role with her grandchildren until her death. Claire becomes functionally overresponsible for her husband, but emotionally and functionally underresponsible for herself and her children. Her mother's overfunctioning role in relationship to her, along with the abusive relationship experienced with her father, has resulted in a complementary sense of incapacity to function for herself that expresses itself in phobias and ultimately alcoholism. Margaret, in turn, overfunctions for mother and "marries" an alcoholic, Margaret's middle sister overfunctions for her father and marries an alcoholic, and the youngest sister marries an overresponsible man and is symptomatic though not alcoholic.

Commonly each overresponsible woman began to take "pride" in her overfunctioning and became perfectionistic, controlling, or giving as an attempt to salvage self-esteem, to cover feelings of inadequacy, and indeed to maintain a pseudo sense of self in a family environment in which all healthy self focus and growth is sacrificed to an obsessive preoccupation with alcohol and the alcoholic. Emotional expressiveness is significantly absent in all family relationships. None of the women in the family are capable of expressing anger openly or directly. They all suffer from chronic depression, underlying guilt, and low self-esteem. They choose partners with whom they have clear one up or one down complementary. If they operate in the one-up position with their partner, it is in the interest of having what is experienced as a valid target on whom to externalize anger. If in the one down position (the youngest sister, or at times Claire) their one down status justifies or permits underresponsibility as well as anger at the person perceived as one up. This drama occurs in a larger context in which it is assumed that males are entitled to power and to having needs met without having to make those needs known explicitly, in which the "appropriate" hierarchical arrangement is one in which the male is one up, and in which all women inherit a legacy of intense guilt if they do not overfunction or, conversely, if they do directly acknowledge their anger or their own desires and feelings.

The family divides into an odd assortment of caretaking "couples," the alliances shifting at times in response to different types of stresses — always the boundaries inappropriate. In a more dysfunctional family, the inappropriately close relationship between Joe and his middle daughter may have become overtly incestuous. As it is, the marital relationship is never primary and the parents are never parents, the children are parents. Even the youngest sister in some way seems to "care take" her mother by providing a demand for focus and attention that helps the mother to avoid the father. It seems clear that the youngest sister functions less and is more sickly because the two older sisters function more.

### Implications for Treatment

This case is a very simplified presentation of patterns of generational progression as they evolved around one family's alcoholism.

In this case, Margaret, the oldest overfunctioning daughter, sought individual therapy. The treatment approach involved use of Bowen family systems therapy (Bowen, 1978; Carter & McGoldrick, 1976) with one individual. At the point that Margaret entered treatment, she was frightened, felt out of control, and desperate because for many years she had coped with her life by overfunctioning, by being a family caretaker, and by dealing with her own needs and feelings by intellectualizing them away. Some exposure to Al-Anon had convinced her that she must detach and limit her involvement with the problems caused by her father's increased drinking. As she began to do this, the family reacted by implying that she was weak and selfish.

As Margaret began slowly to disengage from her overresponsibility within her family she needed equally to struggle with similar issues in the context of her primary relationship. Her major goal was to develop a sense that she had a right to assert her needs, views, and strengths for her own benefit rather than everyone else's. She continually fought the feeling that such behavior was disloyal and would result in her being unloved and abandoned. She felt chronically depressed, felt that nothing she could do would be enough to satisfy her parents or herself, and in general experienced a deep, fatiguing sense of emotional bankruptcy. While it is not within the scope of this paper to present a full discussion of the Bowen approach, the major stages and goals of therapy with Margaret involved the following:

1. Margaret's participation in Al-Anon was encouraged and reinforced. While this is not specifically a directive espoused by Bowen, it is this author's belief that it is only within the context of the AA and Al-Anon programs that clients can encounter a corrective experience that reverses the dysfunctional emotional and interpersonal patterns that evolve in interaction with alcohol or the alcoholic.

2. Consistent with the philosophy of Al-Anon, which encourages self-focus and self-responsibility, Margaret was coached to begin to relinquish the overresponsible role within her family and within her primary relationship. This is long and often tedious work which involves giving directives about specific functional behaviors to relinquish. For instance, Margaret learned to stop buying clothes for her lover or to stop taking complete responsibility for all household chores. With respect to her family of origin, she learned to stop making a three-hour drive to visit every week or to cut back on almost daily phone calls. She learned to stop giving her mother advice about her own drinking or about her father's problems.

Much more at issue, of course, was the level of fusion in the family (lack of a sense of separateness or differentiation) in which Margaret's emotional state was embedded. Margaret worked with a genogram to chart and research family patterns. This helped her to acquire enough emotional distance from her situation to think more objectively about what she wanted from her relationships and how her particular patterns of behavior prevented her from getting it. She was coached to reverse patterns that kept her stuck in emotional overresponsibility. For instance, she was told to begin asking family members to give *her* help and advice rather than continuing to act as the advice giver herself. She began to tell family members about her own feelings of weakness, about her fear that she "couldn't handle" the effects of the progressively worsening drinking. Feeling that she would like Claire to be more giving to her, she wrote letters telling her how much it meant when Claire was giving and responsive. As the crisis in the family worsened, Margaret was able to take a strong position not to act when her youngest sister interrupted her vacation with a plea for her to "do something" about her father's latest binge. Ultimately Margaret arranged for two therapy sessions with her family in which she was able to talk about her feelings, about what was happening in the family and in her own life, and to make direct statements about what she wanted for herself and from her relationships within the family. Very slowly she began to make similar reversals and statements in her primary relationship.

3. As the family began to react to Margaret's changes, a different phase of therapy evolved in which two patterns were notable. First, Margaret's middle sister stepped up her overfunctioning in response to her father's drinking but ultimately followed Margaret's lead and detached as well, and the mother threatened separation. At that point, Margaret's father finally achieved some tenuous sobriety.

As Margaret attempted to reverse her role in her family, she met with much anger and hostility. She went from being in the "hero" role to being in the "scapegoat" role (Wegscheider, 1981). Attempts to talk directly with her mother met with almost total lack of response, and for this reason, this phase of therapy necessitated a more affective, less cognitive approach. Margaret needed to have validated and to grieve the emotional realities of life in an alcoholic family: the very real emotional deprivation, and the inappropriate demands made on her as a child to be an adult rather than to experience acceptance of and response to her dependency. Margaret alternately felt great emptiness and great anger and the process of integrating those two emotional states was a long and very painful one. Margaret gradually realized that the "strengths" she took pride in, competence, intellectual understanding, and focus on achievement, were survival skills that now sometimes blocked her emotional development. They sometimes became overstated attempts to gain a sense of self in a family in which there was little or no validation of her value as a person or as a woman.

4. Margaret began to understand the connections between patterns in her family of origin and her interaction with her lover. Gradually she learned to define her needs and positions separately from those of her lover. Her focus of energy shifted more to herself and she became less entangled in the emotional context of her relationship.

## DISCUSSION AND SUMMARY

Margaret's story is typical of those of women who grow up as female children in alcoholic families. Dependency and responsibility for or focus on others become confused. As a generalization it could be said that women in alcoholic families do more of what women in general are taught to do. They shift from or fail to develop a societally prohibited focus on self to a focus on others. In the face of the significant dysfunction and very real deprivation of the alcoholic family, unmet dependency needs are responded to by an almost total abdication of self—one either focuses totally on the other or one becomes actively abusive of self—that is, one drinks, abuses drugs, overeats, or engages in other forms of self-negating or self-constricting behavior. Margaret is really a mirror image of her alcoholic mother who is a mirror image of her own mother— each represents some combination of either an over or underresponsible response to the same feelings of emptiness, rage, guilt, and worthlessness.

It is typical that Margaret, the overresponsible daughter, rather than her mother, sisters, or father was the person in the family who sought treatment. One benefit of the overresponsible role is that the woman does develop strengths and competencies that provide some measure of self-esteem or some measure of exposure to outside resources that make it feasible on either an emotional or cognitive level for her to seek help. It is typical however, that the client seeks treatment with the covert hope that she can "help" someone else in the family to change.

Women in the underresponsible or alcoholic position usually seek treatment only when others in the environment begin to provide feedback that their behavior is no longer tolerable. Their denial that they have a problem is typically intense and the process of confronting that denial needs to be orchestrated at a slower pace than is true for male alcoholics. Therapists must be cautious about their own tendency to deny or avoid the reality of the woman's substance abuse. Treatment with the alcoholic woman would focus on many of the same issues and goals noted in Margaret's treatment. The important exception is that at least six months of stable sobriety in AA should be required before work on family and interactional patterns is undertaken. Working through feelings of guilt and shame must occur before the alcoholic woman is likely to let go of denial, and the therapist must guard against the alcoholic woman's tendency to step up overresponsible behavior after sobriety in an effort to compensate for guilt and failure. While the overresponsible woman is helped at first to back off from her caretaking role, the alcoholic woman who is underresponsible is coached to assume more appropriate responsibility for self.

The treatment of women in alcoholic systems is best accomplished in a context in which the influence of gender difference is recognized as a significant determinant of adaptive response within the family. The larger social context and the constricting, devalued nature of women's roles are important factors affecting women's attitudes towards and motivation for change. The shift from other focus to self focus is not one that is easily accomplished by women, but ultimately sobriety and the general health of families may depend on it.

## REFERENCES

Babcock, M. & Connor, B. (1981). "Sexism and treatment of the female alcoholic: A review." *Social Work*, 26, 233-238.

Beckman, Linda (1975). "Women alcoholics: A review of social and psychological studies." *Journal of Studies on Alcohol*, 36, 797-825.

Beckman, Linda (1978). "Sex role conflict in alcoholic women: Myth or reality." *Journal of Abnormal Psychology*, 37, 408-417.

Bepko, C. with Krestan, J. (1985). The *Responsibility Trap: A Blueprint for Treating the Alcoholic Family*. New York: Free Press.

Berenson, D. (1976). "Alcohol and the Family System." In P. Guerin (Ed.), *Family Therapy: Theory and Practice*. New York: Gardner Press.

Black, Claudia (1981). *It Will Never Happen to Me*: CO: M.A.C.

Bohman, M., Sigvardsson, S. & Cloninger, C. R. (1981). "Maternal inheritance of alcohol abuse: Cross fostering analysis of adopted women." *Archives of General Psychiatry*, 38, 965-969.

Bowen, Murray (1978). *Family Therapy in Clinical Practice*. New York: Jason Aronson.

Carter, E. & Orfandis, M. McGoldrick (1976). "Family Therapy with One Person and the Family Therapist's Own Family." In P. Guerin, (Ed.), *Family Therapy: Theory and Practice*. New York: Gardner Press.

Corrigan, Eileen (1980). *Alcoholic Women in Treatment*. New York: Oxford University Press.

Cotton, N.S. (1979). "Familial incidence of alcoholism: A Review." *Journal of Studies on Alcohol*, 40, 89-116.

Curlee, J. (1970). "A comparison of male and female patients at an alcoholism treatment center." *Journal of Psychology*, 74,239-247.

Davis, D.I., Berenson, D., Steinglass, P. & Davis, S. (1974). "The adaptive consequences of drinking." *Psychiatry*, 37,209-215.

Elder, T.C. (1973). "Alcoholism and its onset in a population of admitted alcoholics" (an AA study). *British Journal of Addiction*, 68, 291-294.

Gomberg, E.S. (1976). Alcoholism in Women. In B. Kissin &H. Begleiter (Eds.), *The Biology of Alcoholism*, Vol. 4. *Social Aspects of Alcoholism*. New York: Plenum Press.

Gomberg, E.S.L. (1980). "Risk Factors Related to Alcohol Problems Among Women: Proneness and Vulnerability." In *Alcoholism and Alcohol Abuse Among Women: Research Issues*. (NIAAA Research Monograph No. 1, DHEW Publ. No. [ADM] 80-835.) Washington, DC: U.S. Government Printing Office.

Gomberg, E.S.L. & Lisansky, E. (1984). "Antecedents of Alcohol Problems in Women." In S. Wilsnack & L. Beckman (Eds.), *Alcohol Problems in Women*. New York: Guilford Press.

Goodwin, D.W. (1976). *Is Alcoholism Hereditary?* New York: Oxford University Press.

Goodwin, D.W. (1979). "Alcoholism and heredity." *Archives of General Psychiatry*, 36, 57-61.

Greenblatt, M. & Schuckit, M. (Eds.), (1976). *Alcohol Problems in Women and Children*. New York: Grune and Stratton.

Jackson, Joan. (1954). "The adjustment of the family to the crisis of alcoholism." *Quarterly Journal of Studies on Alcohol*, 15, 562-586.

Johnson, P., Armor, D.J., Polich, S. & Stambul, H. (1977). "US Adult Drinking Practices: Time Trends, Social Correlates, and Sex Roles." Prepared for the National Institute on Alcohol Abuse and Alcoholism. (Report No. PB 294-004/AS.) Springfield, VA: U.S. National Technical Information Service.

Morrissey, E.R. (1978). "Alcohol-related problems in adolescents and women." *Postgraduate Medicine*, 64, 111-113.

Sandmaier, M. (1980). *Invisible Alcoholics: Women and Alcohol Abuse in America*. New York: McGraw-Hill.

Wegscheider, Sharon (1981). *Another Chance: Hope and Health for the Alcoholic Family*. Palo Alto, CA: Science and Behavior Books.

Wilsnack, S. (1973). "Sex role identity in female alcoholism." *Journal of Abnormal Psychology*. 82, 253-261.

Wilsnack, S. (1980). "Prevention of Alcohol Problems in Women: Current Status and Research Needs." In *Alcoholism and Alcohol Abuse Among Women: Research Issues*. NIAAA Research Monograph No. 1, U.S. Department of Health, Education, and Welfare, Publication No. ADM-80-835. Washington, DC: U.S. Government Printing Office.

Wilsnack, S. (1982). "Alcohol Abuse and Alcoholism in Women." In E.M. Pattison & E. Kaufman (Eds.), *Encyclopedic Handbook of Alcoholism*. New York: Gardner Press.

Wilsnack, S. & Beckman, L. (1984). *Alcohol Problems in Women*. New York: Guilford Press.

# Lesbian Daughters and Lesbian Mothers: The Crisis of Disclosure from a Family Systems Perspective

Jo-Ann Krestan

**SUMMARY.** Working from a Bowen family systems perspective, a critical aspect of the therapeutic task with lesbian clients is that of coaching them to "come out" in the family of origin. The disclosure of lesbianism, particularly that of a daughter to a mother or a mother to a daughter, is discussed. This article examines the societal context in which a woman makes a lesbian choice and discusses the necessity for disclosure. The particular issues and difficulties involved, the clinical methodology used, and some common results are presented. Case examples illustrate the ideas discussed.

What's a daughter do about a mother?
When she's the apple of her mother's eye?
   Does she make her mother squirm
   By exposing the worm?
Or does she help her mother deny?

        Lyrics from a lesbian musical ©Krestan
        "The Daughter's Song"

Where did I go wrong?
Am I the one to blame?
What was it that I did to her
To bring about this shame?
How did it happen?
How could it possibly be?
That she . . . she . . . she's
So different
From me?

        Lyrics from a lesbian musical ©Krestan
        "The Mother's Song"

Jo-Ann Krestan, MA, is Director, Family Therapy Associates, 718 River Road, Fair Haven, NJ 07701.

*113*

Lesbianism poses questions of difference, and lesbians, like other minorities, share the dilemmas of difference. Difference in its many forms in our society always challenges the assumptions of the similar. Difference informs at the same time that it threatens. And difference, whether of color, of religion, of sexual preference, or merely of opinion, is frequently an invitation to rejection.

There are commonalities which the lesbian shares with other minorities such as vulnerability to discrimination and analogies which may be drawn between lesbianism and the holding of other unpopular views. Nonetheless, being a lesbian is critically different from being a member of a racial or ethnic minority along the dimensions of choice, visibility, and community.

Not only is homosexuality predominantly viewed as deviant rather than variant, but a homosexual choice is *almost always* viewed as a choice whether or not the individual experiences a sense of choice. Therefore, much of society holds homosexuals accountable for their homosexuality. A black person or a Jewish person is not usually held accountable for their blackness or their Jewishness.

When we discuss the concept of lesbian choice we must think through what we mean by lesbian, and what we mean by choice.

The term lesbian describes a woman whose primary emotional and sexual orientation is to other women. The concept of choice is somewhat more complex. John Money (Coleman, 1982) and others believe that sexual preference is set by the age of three. Here, there is clearly no choice. However, as Kinsey noted, the vast majority of people in our society fall somewhere between the extremes of exclusive homosexuality and exclusive heterosexuality. I find it useful to think of a matrix with three intersecting vectors representing sexual preference, emotional preference, and what may be referred to as life-style or role preference. A lesbian choice might for some women be primarily determined by sexual and emotional preference. Alternatively, an individual might minimize her sexual and emotional preference for women because of the importance she accords to a life-style choice involving perceived financial security and children. The point is that the three factors are weighted differently for different individuals. A lesbian choice, then, is one in which these factors are so weighted as to lead to a decision to live as a lesbian.

It is crucial to understand the context within which a woman may make such a lesbian choice. "Lesbian relationships are most importantly relationships between two women in a homophobic and sexist society'' (McCandlish, 1982, p. 71). Our societal context is one in which all women are devalued and relationships between women doubly devalued. And whereas homophobia has always existed in society, our current age is one particularly characterized by the widespread public panic and misinformation surrounding AIDS and the resultant increased fear of homosexuality.

Because of the homophobic and heterosexist context in which a lesbian woman has to live, another critical dimension of choice is the one which relates to invisibility. Unlike most black persons, a lesbian may often "pass" for heterosexual, thereby remaining invisible to the dominant society. However, since a lesbian choice refers to an emotional, sexual, and life-style preference, to have to hide one's lesbianism is to have to hide a major dimension of one's life from view. And yet, revealing one's choice renders one vulnerable not only to attitudinal discrimination but, in many cases, to employment discrimination, and other real and material forms of discrimination which are now illegal when used against other minorities. There have even been recent legislative measures to deny social security benefits to acknowledged homosexuals, and United States immigration policy still excludes homosexuals (O'Leary, 1978).

Historically, other minorities have fought discrimination with the support of their fellows and of their families. Yet, there is a major difference between being a lesbian and being another minority group member.

In the case of a black or a Jew, at least one of her parents, and more commonly both, are also members of that same minority group. A lesbian person, in most cases, comes from a heterosexual family. Thus, the minority status of one of the family members is grossly different from the majority status of the rest of the members. It becomes somewhat easier for the majority members of the family, the heterosexuals, to disassociate themselves from the homosexuality of one of their members, and the inducement to do so is great indeed in view of the dominant homophobic climate.

The discontinuity between the lesbian's minority status and her family's majority status, the invisibility chosen by many of her lesbian peers, and the invisibility that social and economic constraints encourage in her all contribute to an extreme lack of support for the lesbian. Whereas other minorities draw strength from community, the lesbian all too often speaks in a singular voice. Even within the women's movement she has been a minority who has had to fight for inclusion (Abbott, 1978).

The lesbian, then, is perceived as having choice points which other minorities do not have. First, she is commonly perceived as having choice as to whether to be a minority. Again, a black person or a Jewish person is not usually held accountable for their blackness or their Jewishness. Second, she is perceived as having a choice as to whether to disclose that she is a member of that minority.

It is the central thesis of this article that despite the many ramifications of disclosure, the central therapeutic work for a family therapist working from a Bowen systems perspective with a lesbian client is to help the client disclose her lesbianism within her family of origin.

As stated above, lesbianism poses questions of difference. Any individual will, in the course of her life, make certain choices or hold certain beliefs which run counter to the expectations of her family of origin. She will then choose to remain silent about these beliefs in order to avoid the emotional reactivity such beliefs will likely engender in her family (or other emotional systems) or she will choose to define herself and become aware of the reaction of others. Any differentiated stand may elicit initial negative reactions from the family as the forces for emotional togetherness operate almost automatically to restore old balances. The task for the individual then becomes one of deciding whether to hold to her stand or relinquish it. The therapeutic task is to help her make this choice without undue emotional reactivity; in other words, without becoming excessively angry or defensive, without trying to convince others to believe or behave differently, and without cutting off. When it is not possible for an individual to have and express a sense of where she stands on important emotional issues without becoming reactive if other individuals in the family challenge her or try to convince her to be different, then an emotional "cut-off" often ensues in which family members may maintain polite but superficial contact with one another but in which authentic relatedness is not possible. A cut-off deprives the individual of the rich emotional resources of her family of origin and always puts more pressure on the nuclear family which is then in danger of becoming an increasingly closed system.

## REASONS FOR DISCLOSURE

The importance of the client's disclosure of lesbianism in her family of origin cannot be overstated.

Often a lesbian has hidden from herself for many years because it has been difficult to acknowledge thoughts and feelings which would brand her as different and bad. "Coming out" thus refers first to an internal process of acknowledgment and second to an interactional process.

> Every time a homosexual denies the validity of his feelings or restrains himself from expressing, he does a small hurt to himself. He turns his energies inward and suppresses his own vitality. The effect may be scarcely noticeable: joy may be a little less keen, happiness slightly subdued, he may simply feel a little run down, a little less tall. Over the years, these tiny denials have a cumulative effect. (Fisher, 1972, p. 249)

Fisher here is writing about male homosexuals. Certainly his observations apply even more keenly to lesbians, who as women, have been socialized to deny their feelings, to adapt to others' desires, always to put themselves last, and often in the process put themselves down. The incidence of depression in women alone is testament to this process of devaluing self (Braverman, 1986). Surely lesbians, their self-esteem already endangered by being women in a sexist society, are extremely vulnerable to internalizing homophobia, and accepting society's message that something is wrong with them. Even the fact that men are more punished for sissy behavior than women are for tomboy behavior, testifies to the importance to society of the male role.

Don Clark says, "It is best to work on the assumption that you cannot hold the secret of your Gay identity forever. Each time you pretend to be non-Gay when you are Gay, you give yourself a silent, irrational message that it is wrong or bad to be the person you are" (Clark, 1977, p. 62). Disclosure serves to counteract this message. To disclose is to rechannel the energy that heretofore has been diverted into holding secrets, and to have that energy available for self.

On a personal level, disclosure is an important statement to oneself that one is unwilling to accept the negative messages that society gives about lesbianism. On a family level, disclosure opens up the possibility of authentic personal relationships with family members. It is difficult at best to have an authentic relationship when one is concentrating energy on changing pronouns in conversation, disguising destinations, and the way in which time is spent; in short, hiding and thereby disowning the self. Differentiation of self involves taking the risk of being fully who one is and thereby entering into honest relationship to others. Lack of differentiation around any issue in a family system manifests itself by a high degree of emotional reactivity around the issue, by taking refuge from that reactivity in silence or secret holding, and by even greater emotional cut-off. Secrets deprive people of rich emotional resources within the family (Karpel, 1980).

Another very important reason for counseling disclosure as part of the continuing work of differentiating self from one's family of origin is that lesbian relationships are particularly prone to becoming closed systems, and closed systems develop problems. Lesbian partners tend to fuse because they have rigidified their boundaries in an attempt to survive in a society which invalidates their boundaries (Krestan & Bepko, 1980).

> It appears, then, that fusion issues within the relationship may result in part from attempts by the couple to maintain the subsystem within a larger system whose feedback about their relationship would constantly suggest that they dissolve it . . . Because the lesbian or homosexual couple must spend excessive amounts of energy defining their boundaries in order to maintain their relatedness and private space in the face of countervailing forces, energy spent in more individual behavior may tip the balance of the relationship toward dissolution. In the homosexual couple, individuation is not countered by external forces supporting the survival of the "marriage." It is as though the heterosexual pair operates in an energy field of centrifugal force and the homosexual pair operates in a field of centripetal force. (Krestan & Bepko, 1980, pp. 278-279)

When gay people are, in any way, cut-off from the rest of society, they are vulnerable to the kinds of difficulties which often plague closed systems. Some of these difficulties include relationship problems, chemical dependency, and depression.

The most important cut-off is from the lesbian's family of origin, or in the case of a lesbian mother from her children. For most minorities, family is a refuge, a sanctuary, a place where they can be nourished and feel accepted for themselves. But even the decision as to where to spend important holidays is a difficult one for many lesbians who are in a relationship, a difficulty compounded by secrecy if they have not "come out" to their families.

In summary, then, disclosure is important to the lesbian in order for her to counteract her tendency to internalize the homophobic message of society, in order for her to build authentic personal relationships with family members, and in order to avoid the pressure to form an increasingly closed system with her lover and other gay friends that is intensified by secrecy.

## COACHING THE DISCLOSURE

Carter and McGoldrick summarize the process of coaching an individual to differentiate as including five phases. These phases are "the engagement of the client in the process; the teaching or planning phase; the re-entry; the work; and the follow-through" (Carter & McGoldrick, 1976, p. 203).

Engagement of the client involves helping the client to understand the importance of the differentiation work. Although all efforts at differentiation create initial anxiety, "coming out" is a highly specialized instance of differentiation and provokes particular anxiety.

It is important to be mindful of where the client is in terms of acceptance of her lesbian identity and the overall coming out process, as well as in terms of her overall differentiation of self. For example, one would not urge an adult client who has just recently become aware of lesbian feelings or who has not yet been able to sustain financial independence from her family of origin, to discuss her lesbianism with her mother. Such a discussion might be a way of her seeking some external validation, but it is not a way suggestive of individuation.

Ideally, the lesbian client should have disclosed her lesbianism first to people who will definitely accept it rather than making the first disclosure to family. Eli Coleman (1982) makes the point that selectivity in terms of to whom to first disclose is crucial because of the vulnerability of the self-concept during the coming-out phase.

Events such as a lover's impatience with the client's remaining in the closet, or a family life cycle marker such as a heterosexual wedding, may trigger the desire for the client to come out (Roth & Murphy, 1986). I believe that the therapist need not, and should not wait for a natural life cycle event to trigger the desire for disclosure, but should take the position that disclosure to one's immediate family should be planful but should always be a goal of the therapeutic work.

It is often difficult for clients to see that disclosure will be helpful. The client may feel that disclosure will "kill" a parent, or cause a child to reject her, or cause peer problems such as rejection and gossip for her children.

There are almost always concerns as to how holidays and other important family rituals will be handled once other family members know about the lesbianism. Will lovers be invited, what will the seating arrangements be, who will go to the rehearsal dinner for a wedding? Sibling reactions are often feared. Perhaps a lesbian's sister will now ask her to relinquish being guardian for her children. There is no etiquette book to guide relatives of the lesbian or the lesbian herself as to the proper social protocol for even such a basic requirement as how to make a polite introduction of the lesbian's partner. Is she to be introduced as a partner, friend, roommate, lover? Should she be given a Christmas gift? The overriding concern about disclosure, of course, is the fear of loss of relationship. The therapist must be committed to the belief that suppression of self will ultimately be more likely to lead to loss of relatedness than will disclosure.

Where the lesbian has children, custody issues also become a very real and highly justifiable concern. When even the charge of lesbianism is increasingly being used by men in custody disputes, and when men are increasingly winning custody of small children, it must be acknowledged that lesbianism constitutes a real danger to the woman in divorce litigation.

As a therapist coaching self-disclosure as a critical part of the process of differentiation of self, one must be utterly convinced that secrets and covertness lead to trouble. Or, as Rita Mae Brown (1983) states in her lesbian novel, "We are as sick, as we are secret."

Timing, however, is important. One would not choose another family member's important day, like a birthday or anniversary, to disclose. In general, it is best for the lesbian client to set a time to talk with her mother or her daughter individually. She may choose to come out first to a sibling. In that case, she should be coached not to ask the confidante to hold a secret indefinitely, but rather to give her a little lead time to tell other family members herself, and then to essentially give the others her permission to discuss the lesbianism among themselves.

When lesbians do not think through the disclosure, it may come out in anger or as a plea for understanding which then is an apology for and a discount of the lesbianism, or it may even slip out in the form of letters left lying around (Cordova, 1975).

Since one purpose of disclosure is to open a family system up, it is crucial that the client choose words that will not be so toxic as to immediately shut a system down. I believe it is ultimately important for the client to use the word lesbian to herself and to others because using euphemisms is a way of disowning and discounting. Nonetheless, in the first disclosure to a mother or a daughter it is important to take the individual family's style into account and to say things in a way which seeks to minimize any shock value. The client should know which words will be least toxic in her family of origin. Of course, even more crucially, the attitude of the client will help to either defuse the toxicity of the issue or escalate it. An example of a calm disclosure might be:

> There's been something about myself that I have wanted to share with you. For some time I have known that I am more attracted to women that I am to men. You have commented on the fact that Jane and I seem to always do things together. I've wanted you to know that she is not just my best friend but also my life partner. I know that you have always wanted my happiness and well-being and although I know that what I'm saying might worry you, it is important to me for you to know that since I have acknowledged my homosexual feelings to myself, I have felt happier and surer of myself than I have in a long time.

It is important to coach the client to expect an initial reaction of hurt, shock, and anger on the part of her mother or her daughter, and to coach her to wait out the reaction. Predicting some of the common reactions can help to alleviate the client's anxiety and she should be reminded that the family will go through a process of acknowledging her lesbianism just as she herself has had to go through such a process. It is also important to point out that her family does not need to approve of everything about her, just as she surely will not approve of everything about them. What is necessary is mutual respect for difference.

## COMMON CONCERNS
## OF MOTHERS AND DAUGHTERS

Mothers are typically the repositories of most family secrets with the exception of incest. They may be expected to have an initial reaction of hurt and self-blame, and somewhat less frequently they respond with tremendous anger. Often they ask their daughter not to tell other family members because "it would kill your grandmother," or "your father hasn't been well."

Although they are usually concerned, deep-down, for their daughter's happiness, mothers may initially vacillate between self-recrimination and blaming their daughter for hurting them. It is important to remember that mothers have been socialized as women too. They have been taught to believe that a woman cannot be happy or safe or secure without a man. They are frightened for their daughters. They have also been socialized to believe that the emotional relationships of all family members are their responsibility so it is natural that when their daughter chooses primary relationships to women, they may themselves feel that they have failed in their role as a mother.

Daughters, in my clinical experience, tend to have more difficulty with the lesbianism of their mothers than do boys, particularly if they are adolescent at the time of disclosure. They are concerned about the reactions of their peers, as kids hate to be thought of as "different." Also, daughters in adolescence are often struggling with their own sexual identity. The lesbianism of mother may make the daughter question her own adequacy as a female. A daughter may also fear that she will turn out to be a lesbian.

Perhaps, most importantly, one must recognize and prepare one's client for the mutual grieving process which must take place between mothers and daughters. Women who are heterosexual almost always have a primary emotional attachment to another woman as a friend, and the mother daughter attachment is also often a very strong, ambivalent and emotionally charged one. These primary emotional attachments between women are not disturbed or threatened by attachments to men. However, when a lesbian "comes out" as a lesbian, it does involve more of a loss for her mother, her daughter, and her heterosexual best friend than if she announced an attachment to a man. Some mothers and daughters will actually express their jealousy overtly.

Grief, then, is attached to the loss of primacy. But grief also has to do with the mutual recognition of difference. That recognition involves a dissolution of illusion, collapse of any idealization of each other that may have taken place, a recognition of separateness. And from that grief people can be helped to go beyond into a new, more honest level of relationship. But it takes time. It is a process.

## CASES

### Case 1

Margaret, a young woman in her early 20s, had seen the therapist a few times when she was a freshman in college as part of family therapy sessions with her mother and stepfather. She recontacted the therapist a few years later to come in with her mother. In the first session, Margaret revealed that she had told her mother several months before that she was thinking about a lesbian relationship with a woman. Her mother, in their next visit, listed several logical reasons why Margaret shouldn't pursue that line of thinking, and Margaret informed her mother that it was too late, that she, in fact, had become involved in a lesbian relationship. This disclosure was made following a lunch date between Margaret and her mother to which Margaret had invited her lover, but at which she had introduced her lover as her roommate.

Margaret's mother was furious, and the therapeutic work concentrated on helping her and Margaret talk through the issues. The mother's fury included her feeling that she had been manipulated, but it became clear that there probably would have been no good way for Margaret to tell her of her lesbianism. The mother reacted to the lesbianism as though it were a direct insult leveled by Margaret at her. She stated that she felt that the lesbianism would destroy Margaret's relationship with the entire family and she demanded that Margaret not tell any other family members. She was furious at the implications for herself and expressed concern about how she would deal with her own friends. Her blaming of self focused on her having been "too liberal a parent." The mother's politics were liberal, and she had been active in supporting the local chapter of Planned Parenthood and considered herself a feminist. She blamed herself for having shown her children all aspects of life without condemning anyone or any one type of behavior.

Margaret remained very non-reactive despite her mother's rage and overt statements that she could no longer have much of a relationship with Margaret.

Margaret assured her mother that she loved her and knew that they could have a relationship, that her mother could learn to understand through loving her. The mother asserted that she would never understand and did not want a relationship.

The work continued in the above vein for three or four sessions which were held at intervals of a few weeks each. Consistently, the therapist reframed the mother's anger as loss, and worked to help the daughter try to remain emotionally connected to her mother without personalizing her mother's reaction.

Ultimately, the daughter recognized that both were grieving the loss of the dream of fusion and the loss of the image of one another that each had held. Margaret had idealized her mother's liberalism and had to grieve her mother's inconsistency between stated belief and practice without seeing it as hypocrisy, and her mother had to grieve the loss of the dream of her eldest daughter's eventual marriage. It took three years and much additional family work on everyone's part, including other issues for mother and daughter to rebuild their relationship. However, they were able to do so. In fact, two years later, when Margaret was diagnosed with a potentially life-threatening illness, her mother and her lover were readily able to share the necessary caretaking responsibilities.

## Case 2

In the second case, therapeutic work had been done with the lesbian client to prepare her for talking with her mother, but, as is often the case, her mother precipitated the timing. Joan had brought friends around to the house where she was temporarily renting a room from her mother while finishing graduate school evenings.

One night Joan recognized by the look on her mother's face that something was gravely wrong. When she questioned her mother, her mother said that Joan knew what was wrong. Joan asked whether her mother was talking about her life style. Her mother angrily said that she was indeed talking about her life style. "You're a lesbian, aren't you?" Joan admitted that she was. Joan's mother then wept, said that it wasn't normal, and asked how Joan could have done this to her, asking what she had done wrong. She went on to say, "First your sister, then your father, then your brother, and now you're a lesbian." Joan's sister had died young, her father had committed suicide, and her brother is a drug addict. "I have nothing to live for. I should stop taking my medication."

Joan is a well-educated, well-respected professional with many friends. She told her mother that she was happy, that she felt she had accomplished a great deal with her life so far, and, most importantly, she was able to let her mother have her reaction without becoming defensive. In fact, she put her arms around her mother for the first time in years and held her, although her mother continued to be hysterical. In the morning, her mother offered a very quiet apology.

These two cases were selected for brief comment because in each case, despite the daughter's careful thought and relatively nonreactive disclosure of her lesbianism, the mother's reactions were initially very, very angry and hurt. The continuing work of connection fell to the daughters, and took years. Neither mother is likely to ever fully accept the lesbianism. Nonetheless, the work of differentiation rightly belongs to the daughters, and if each can maintain a focus on self and accept her mother for who she is, emotional cutoffs will not be necessary. Both also illustrated a critical principle in differentiation work. The differentiating individual must be able to sit through the reactivity of the other person without becoming reactive herself, blaming or justifying. The temptation to cut off is strong when reactivity on the part of the family continues at a high level, and sometimes it is necessary to coach clients to back off some and create some temporary distance.

## Case 3

Susan who discovered her lesbianism in her forties after 25 years of marriage and three children, told her mother early on that she was homosexual. She made the disclosure calmly at the time of her divorce, but her mother refused to discuss it. For four years Susan's mother and father refused to visit her home, where she lived with her lover and her children, refused to call her except at the office, stopped calling their grandchildren, and sent all of the children's mail to Susan's office address. Susan struggled with ways of reopening an issue which her mother clearly did not want to discuss. Finally, when her mother invited her and the children to her house on a Saturday night, of course excluding Susan's partner, Susan decided that the time was right to reopen the issue. First she told her mother that she would be glad to accept the invitation but that she did things with her partner on Saturday nights. At that point, Susan's mother said that maybe she could accept Susan's homosexuality if only she did not have children, but that she felt terrible for the children and felt that Susan was not showing responsibility toward her children because she was a lesbian. At that point Susan calmly stated, "I really have to tell you that for the last three years I have not felt that you are fulfilling your responsibility as a grandparent." She reminded her mother of the cards and calls sent to the office and of her parent's refusal to visit her home.

At the end, Susan's mother said quietly, "I have no defense." Susan went on to say that she did have a family, and that she is more comfortable with herself than she has ever been in her life. I believe that it is likely that Susan's parents will visit her home in the near future.

This last example illustrates the necessity for a lesbian to make a firm stand. Were she to withhold her feelings from her mother, a cut-off would ensue. Yet, she is to be commended for the nonaccusatory way in which she gave her mother feedback and her willingness to listen to her mother's feelings. The long-term work really focuses on keeping the system open.

## Case 4

When Carol came out to her 16-year-old daughter, it was in a therapy session after many sessions of careful preparation and rehearsal. Still, the anxiety was extremely high. The therapist stated that there had been a lot of changes since the marital separation, and that she was sure that Nancy, the daughter, knew that her father was very upset about her mother. The statement was then made that there might be questions that Nancy had been wanting to ask, and the therapist asked Carol if it was alright for Nancy to ask anything she wanted to. When Carol gave permission, Nancy asked if Carol and Gloria were more than just friends. Part of the session was subsequently spent alone with Nancy. In that part of the session, Nancy indicated that she had been wondering for some time but was afraid to ask for fear of hurting her mother. She also indicated more discomfort with the lesbianism than she shared in front of the mother, voicing some question as to whether it meant that she would turn out gay. Her concern focused most, however, on her mother's choice of partner. She preferred her mother to be with one particular woman who didn't "look it" as much as her mother's current friend did. When questioned more about this, it was clear that if someone "looked it," Nancy inevitably thought about sex and wondered what it was like between two women, and that thought made her uncomfortable.

The inevitable thinking about sex is in part, I believe, a reaction to the media treatment of homosexuality as a statement of sexual preference rather than an emotional and sexual orientation. Because of this association with sex, the lines between identity and privacy are often somewhat ambiguous. Bok (1984) sheds some light on the distinction between the two. "I shall define privacy as the condition of being protected from unwanted access by others . . . secrecy guards, then, the central aspects of secrecy" (Bok, 1984, p. 10-11). Privacy, then, is a part of secrecy. With the secret of lesbianism, however, relinquishing the secret also means making oneself vulnerable to invasions of privacy primarily, I believe, because lesbianism is viewed through such a sexual lens. Many a lesbian woman expresses concern about showing any physical affection once she has "come out" because what would have been a normative gesture between women in our culture is quickly apt to be framed as a sexual overture once people know about her lesbianism.

Likewise, both mothers and daughters, when they are the confidante of the other's lesbianism, frequently ask questions about every woman friend the lesbian has, and such curiosity, while perhaps part of an attempt to understand, nonetheless is experienced usually by the lesbian as unwontedly intrusive.

## Case 5

When Eileen came out to her adolescent daughter Sheila, Sheila's reaction was exceedingly angry. The only girl in a family of six, Sheila had been accustomed to a rather special relationship with her mother following her parents' divorce. When Eileen attempted to set ordinary limits on Sheila's behavior and also limits around her privacy such as leaving her bedroom door shut when her lover was there for the weekend, Sheila reacted with rage and Eileen began to find things missing from her bedroom and from her purse. Sheila also behaved obnoxiously to Eileen's lover.

Eileen's husband knew of her lesbianism but told her that if she was sexually active he would disclose her lesbianism to her parish priest and to her parents, neither of whom yet knew. Sheila, out of anger at her mother, told her father that another woman was spending weekends at the house. Eileen then made the disclosure to her parents before she felt quite ready. To her surprise, although they were not happy about her lesbianism, they were very supportive and assured her that they loved her. They then began including Eileen's lover in any family gatherings. Sheila, however, could not resolve the issue comfortably and opted to live with her father. At this writing, she is negotiating to come back.

## SUMMARY

What these case examples have in common is the difficulty that many mothers and daughters have with the disclosure of lesbianism. I do not believe that this difficulty can be viewed separately from the societal context in which it exists. Today, many heterosexual women are seeking to redefine their roles. However, although many young women are choosing to remain single longer, the redefinition of role for the heterosexual woman still takes place within a relational context—marriage—which is normative. A lesbian woman's struggle to define herself takes place within a context defined as deviant. She is in many ways an invisible woman for whom no relational rules exist.

I believe that all persons need to define themselves in a way which owns their own power, to differentiate a self—distinguishable from their familial, social, ethnic, and cultural context. This differentiation is necessary if women are to function as mature, responsible adults who can direct their own course in life, and yet enter into intimate relationships with other adults.

Such differentiation, however, has traditionally been socially sanctioned, modeled, and reinforced for men, but punished in women. Therefore, for any woman to differentiate is to depart from the culturally prescribed sex role expectations of the larger culture. It is not surprising that the differentiation which is required for a woman to make a lesbian choice may be perceived as dangerous. Women who do not define themselves through their relationship with men but rather through their relationship to other women, or "the woman-identified-woman" (Bunch, 1978) pose particular threats to more traditional notions of who women are. If the continuing history of the relationship of lesbianism to feminism has been the story of an intense struggle to make lesbian equal rights a legitimate feminist issue, then how much more difficult and dangerous does it seem for lesbianism to be introduced as an issue to be discussed between mothers and daughters? Mothers and daughters have always had to hide from themselves and from each other, as women have hidden through the years in depression, alcoholism, and other problems. They have hidden from each other, and, more sadly, they have hidden from themselves.

To counsel a lesbian to disclose her lesbianism is to counsel her to disclose herself in a context which labels that self as deviant. But the importance of disclosure of women to women is much larger than the issue of lesbianism. As women begin to be free to be themselves with each other, they can begin to overcome the effects of a society which silences them. It is not just lesbian women who must learn to be themselves without the need for self-justification. All women need to learn to "come out."

## REFERENCES

Abbott, S. (1978). Lesbians and the women's movement. In G. Vida (Ed.), *Our right to love: A lesbian resource book*. Englewood Cliffs, NJ: Prentice-Hall.

Berzon, B. (1979). Developing a positive gay identity. In B. Berzon & R. Leighton (Eds.), *Positively gay*. Millbae, CA: Celestial Arts.

Bok, S. (1984). *Secrets: On the ethics of concealment and revelation*. New York: Vintage Books.

Braverman, L. (1986). The depressed woman in context: A feminist family therapist's analysis. In M. Ault-Riché & J. C. Hansen (Eds.), *Women and family therapy*. Rockville, MD: Aspen Systems Corporation.

Brown, R. M. (1983). *Sudden death*. New York: Bantam Books.

Bunch, C. (1978). Lesbian-feminist theory. In G. Vida (Ed.), *Our right to love: A lesbian resource book*. Englewood Cliffs, NJ: Prentice-Hall.

Carter, E. & Orfanidis, M. (1976). Family therapy with one person and the family therapist's own family. In P. Guerin (Ed.), *Family therapy: Theory and practice*. New York: Gardner Press.

Clark, D. (1977). *Loving someone gay*. Millbrae, CA: Celestial Arts.

Coleman, E. (1982). Developmental stages of the coming out process. In J. C. Gonsiorek (Ed.), *Homosexuality and psychotherapy*. New York: Haworth Press.

Cordova, J. (1975). How to come out without being thrown out. In K. Jay & A. Young (Eds.), *After you're out*. New York: Links Books.

Fisher, P. (1972). *The gay mystique*. New York: Stein & Day.

Karpel, M. (1980). Family secrets: I. Conceptual and ethical issues in the relational context. II. Ethical and practical considerations in therapeutic management. *Family process*, 19, 295-306.

Krestan, J. & Bepko, C. (1980). The problem of fusion in the lesbian relationship. *Family process*, 19, 277-289.

McCandlish, B. M. (1982). Therapeutic issues with lesbian couples. In J. C.

Gonsiorek (Ed.), *Homosexuality and psychotherapy*. New York: Haworth Press.

O'Leary, J. (1978). Legal problems and remedies. In G. Vida (Ed.), *Our right to love: A lesbian resource book*. Englewood Cliffs, NJ: Prentice-Hall.

Roth, S. & Murphy, B. C. (1986). Therapeutic work with lesbian clients: A systemic therapy view. In M. Ault-Riché & J. C. Hansen (Eds.), *Women and family therapy*. Rockville, MD: Aspen Systems Corporation.

# Women and Eating Disorders

Richard C. Schwartz
Mary Jo Barrett

**SUMMARY.** This paper presents a view of eating disorders that highlights the interdependent nature of: the subordinate position of women in our society; our culture's emphasis on thinness and dieting; the way these cultural extremes are reflected in eating disordered families; and finally the way these extremes are reflected in the internal processes of anorexic and bulimic women. This multi-level perspective is illustrated with a case example.

The eating disorders of anorexia nervosa (self-starvation) and bulimia (repeated episodes of bingeing food and subsequent purging of the food) are widely considered to be "women's problems." By most reports, between 80% and 90% of those who suffer from either anorexia or bulimia are women (DSM III).

The authors have studied eating disordered clients, their families, and their sociocultural contexts for the past six years. We now see anorexia nervosa and bulimia not simply as aberrant sets of eating habits but as rigid and extreme patterns of thinking, feeling, and interacting with others. These patterns, we have found, are established within the individual's familial and sociocultural contexts. Consequently, these eating disorders cannot be understood or treated effectively without examining these contexts, both in general and with respect to the individual client.

We will briefly describe the sociocultural, familial, and individual factors, which contribute to the creation of the eating disorders of anorexia nervosa and bulimia and how these disorders function for women. In conclusion, we will summarize our treatment model through a clinical case example.

Richard C. Schwartz is Coordinator of Training and Research, Family Systems Program, Institute for Juvenile Research, 907 S. Wolcott, Chicago, IL 60612. Mary Jo Barrett is Director of Midwest Family Resource, 6 North Michigan, #1502, Chicago, IL 60602.

## CONTRIBUTING FACTORS

Both men and women receive messages from society and their families that both help create and explain their behaviors. The messages for the two sexes tend to be very different in content but they do teach both men and women how to think, how to feel, how to treat others, how to expect to be treated by others, how to appear physically, and even how to eat. It then becomes the task of the individual to sort through all these similar or conflicting messages and evolve into a person.

### Sociocultural Factors

For clarity of presentation the following three sociocultural factors are described as discrete and separate phenomena. They are, however, highly interrelated and tend to perpetuate each other's existence. The factors discussed are:

— the subordinate position of women in society;
— the role of nurturer and caretaker occupied by women; and
— the pressure placed on women to be physically attractive and thin.

First, women have historically occupied a subordinate position in society. Social norms have taught women to expect limited power and to be satisfied with limited control over their own lives as well as the lives of others. Women are not encouraged to be assertive or direct in their communication, rather they learn to be passive and covert. They are implicitly asked to create the illusion of dependence. Illusion, because while they are supposed to be subordinate and dependent, in reality they are expected to meet their own needs and the needs of others.

A number of authors have tied the subordinate and illusionary position of women in society to women's eating disorders (Orbach, 1978; Wooley & Wooley, 1980; Boskind, White & White, 1983; Polivy & Herman, 1983; Bennett & Gavin, 1982). Bulimia and anorexia nervosa help women satisfy the societal mandate of subordination. Being anorectic or bulimic makes one feel and appear inadequate. Sufferers of both disorders often find themselves in need of physical care. Yet, being bulimic or anorectic is very powerful. No one can control their eating or their purging. The disorders are a very indirect method of gaining power and control over one's life. Consequently, eating disorders maintain both the position of the dependent person in need of constant care and attention and the position of powerful and overcontrolling demagogue. This indirect method of gaining power and control, while remaining subordinate is congruent with the societal message that women are taught.

The second sociocultural factor influencing women with eating disorders is the injunction to be unselfish, self-sacrificing, and to think of others first. Women are to caretake the emotional, physical, social, spiritual, and many times the material needs of others, while simultaneously denying their own needs.

How can a woman nurture others while at the same time deny her own needs? Both anorexia and bulimia can serve these functions for women. A woman can perform overresponsible and sacrificial tasks and only reward herself sparingly. The physical numbing effect that results from both self-starvation and purging creates a denial system that helps a person deny hunger, feelings, and needs. Consequently, she can take care of others' needs and deny her own.

The final sociocultural influence is the ideal that the attractive woman is thin. Many women are taught by society and their families that success, intimacy, security, and life satisfaction are gained through becoming and staying thin and attractive. Consequently, this becomes a major life goal.

The abhorrence of fat and worship of thin has several consequences. One consequence is the struggle it creates between body and will; the will to be thin and the body's need for sustenance. During this struggle a woman must dissociate from her body's hunger and satiation signals. Because this dissociation is often futile, her low sense of control in the world is accentuated. (Polivy & Herman, 1983; Bennett & Gavin, 1982). In cases where the "will" wins the struggle and hunger is conquered, a woman may cling to this new power and perfection and become anorectic. If the deprived dieter launches into a binge, she hates herself for the transgression and purges as a way to simultaneously punish herself and reach her goal of perfect thinness. In either case, both anorexia nervosa and bulimia help a woman get closer to her goals of thinness and attractiveness.

## Familial Factors

The sociocultural factors previously described are reflected and often exaggerated in the values and interactions of the families of anorexics and bulimics. In the families we studied, we found the messages regarding the sociocultural factors varied depending on the families close identification with either a traditional "ethnic" background or an "americanized" tradition (Schwartz et al., 1985). In both "ethnic" and "americanized" families there is a sense that men are or should be more valuable, powerful, or competent than women; and that a woman's value or competence only comes through her association with a man. Many of these families are male-dominated in the sense that the father made the important decisions, was idealized by other family members, and that there existed among family members a competitive struggle for his approval. Even in the cases where the father had fallen from grace, for example through alcohol or the sexual abuse of a daughter, the families maintained their male orientation and found excuses for the father's behavior. Thus, in anorectic and bulimic families the approval of men is stressed as one of the daughter's goals.

In both the "ethnic" and "americanized" families we perceived a high degree of conflict, with no perceivable method of conflict resolution. Families with an anorectic daughter kept their conflict extremely covert. They attempted to communicate to the outside world that their family was problem free. On the other hand, families with a bulimic member had extreme overt conflict that often lasted for years. In either case, the covert or overt conflicts never were resolved.

The two types of families differ in some areas. In the "americanized" families there is a great emphasis on achievement, success, and perfection according to male standards. The clients in these families are told they have a great potential talent that must be realized. The "americanized" families also have an extreme concern about vogue appearance, including dress and pressure to be thin. The pressure of being perfect for your father through achievement, combined with the desire to please mother through nurturing skills, and attending to the messages of denial, and nonaggressive selflessness, in order to satisfy societal norms creates intense conflicts that the daughter believes she must resolve.

In the more "ethnic" families, vogue appearance and high achievement are downplayed, while values of loyalty to the family and the maintenance of traditional woman's roles are stressed. Serving others, perfecting domestic skills, raising children, and staying close to home are the predominant, rigidly instilled values. In these families, food often becomes a symbolic language for defining relationships. Anger or rebellion can be expressed by either not eating or vomiting the parent's food—rejecting the mother by rejecting her food and simultaneously rejecting the father in his role of "bread winner."

We found that a large number of clients, in both types of families, were intensely worried about the well-being of their parents or their parents' relationship whether married, separated, or divorced. The daughter either becomes involved in the marital issues directly or attempts to satisfy one or both parents because they are not receiving satisfaction from their spouse. This involvement can exist whether the child is living inside or outside of the home. In such cases, the eating problems provide a distraction from other issues for both parent and child, an excuse for not becoming autonomous or leaving home, and a reason for the parents to become more involved in their child's life and less involved in their marriage. In other words, anorexia nervosa and bulimia give both the parents and the daughter avenues to be protective and protected.

Eating disordered families are microcosms of the extremes of American and ethnic macrocosms. As Jules Henry (1963) has observed, "Every family . . . is somewhat different from every other, the difference consisting in the manner in which each develops its own version of the general cultural configuration" (p. 7). The difference between eating disordered families and other families lies in the way the values and themes of society have become rigid and polarized.

### Individual Factors

Society and families communicate conflicting messages to the individual woman. It is quite a burden for a woman to make decisions regarding her life when so much is demanded of her. She has many internalized conflicts to resolve and yet has no model from either society or her family to illustrate conflict resolution. What we have discovered is that anorectics and bulimics participate in an intrapsychic dialogue with respect to the extreme values and messages. The first author (Schwartz, 1986) has traced the interactional patterns of these internalized "parts" or "voices" and found that each theme of the family is represented by a "part" of the client. For example, most clients have a part that tells them to achieve and is critical when they do not. Another part of themselves is very concerned regarding their appearance and the way they appear to others, particularly men, and will tell them they are too fat and do not look good. While another part might also be telling the woman that she looks fine and that there are more important aspects of self.

Commonly, another internalized part worries about the parents' marriage and tells them to be sacrificial. Yet there is almost always the part that tells the anorectic or bulimic to avoid conflict if possible because there is no resolution. These examples illustrate only a few of the potential messages with which a woman struggles.

Other internalized efforts, such as achieving autonomy and intimacy outside the family or achieving nontraditional goals, are overridden by the rigid messages of society and family. These eating disordered women do possess the "parts" that would choose to be functional. The resolution between the different internalized "parts" becomes too overwhelming and unresolvable. Consequently, the dysfunctional "part" wins over the functional.

Bulimia and anorexia nervosa resolve conflict and avoid conflict at the same time. When the woman is eating and purging or starving herself she cannot attend to the internalized struggle that exists. She is not physically or emotionally capable of making decisions or trusting the decisions she does make. When she finds herself in an internal or external context where she is unhappy but feels powerless to change, she can distract herself through thoughts or actions concerning food and eating. The eating disorders allow her to be deaf to the parts struggling within her. She literally and figuratively numbs herself to the conflicting messages she receives and consequently they are resolved for the moment. When the same conflict or a new one emerges the eating disorder sequence begins again.

## TREATMENT MODEL

The treatment model presented was designed to address all three contextual factors: sociocultural, familial, and individual. The model takes into consideration that bulimia and anorexia nervosa function very efficiently for women and their families. Because the eating disorders are reinforced by all three contexts and help women maintain their sense of self and sense of roles, they are very difficult symptoms to treat.

The primary concepts for the treatment model are influenced by both the structural (Minuchin, 1974; Minuchin & Fishman, 1981; Minuchin et al., 1978) and the strategic (Fisch, Weakland, & Segal, 1982; Haley, 1976; Madanes, 1981) schools of family therapy. The model is composed of three stages: (1) creating a context for change; (2) challenging patterns and expanding alternatives; and (3) consolidation. The interventions of each stage are aimed at restructuring the woman's dysfunctional interactions with food, self and others so that she is no longer continuing patterns that maintain anorexia nervosa or bulimia.

To illustrate the treatment model we have included the following case example. This illustration highlights the aspects of treatment which are most related to the client's struggle as she attempts to define and maintain herself as a woman.

## CASE EXAMPLE

Janet was a college freshman when her mother first contacted the agency for therapy. She was in school in Chicago and her family lived in another state. In her first three months of school she had lost 35 pounds. When she began treatment, Janet was five feet six inches and weighed 74 pounds.

Janet's father was a successful lawyer with his own firm and her mother, currently a homemaker, had been a professor of literature. Janet was a prelaw student, but her interests were in Italian art history. She had two older sisters and an older brother.

### Creating a Context for Change

The first sessions were geared toward helping Janet feel more responsible for and in control of the most immediate decisions in her life – those related to her eating. After having her see a medical doctor with whom we collaborate, it was determined that hospitalization was not necessary if she was closely monitored. Janet and her family were told that as long as her weight or electrolytes did not fall, she would not be hospitalized and she was to be in charge of what she ate. We had no interest in forcing her to gain weight and she, no doubt, had good reasons not to gain; reasons which we would explore before weight gain would be discussed in treatment.

After these initial sessions, designed to defuse power struggles between the therapist, Janet, and her family, treatment proceeded with Janet being seen individually once a week and her family coming to sessions once a month. This pattern of sessions varied over the course of treatment.

In the individual sessions, treatment focused on the meaning of Janet's anorexia, to her. To help her become acutely aware of the context of her relationship to food she was asked to keep a journal. The journal was to log the times she thought about food, when she prepared food for others, when she denied herself food, and the times she allowed herself to eat food. She was to track for each occasion where she was, who she was with, what was happening at that point and in the recent past, and what she was feeling and thinking. She was not to alter her eating in any way, but to simply become aware of it. As she brought in entries from the journal, we used them to build the themes for treatment. For example, the themes of how the anorexia assisted her in denying the changes she wanted in her relationships, in school, and in her life in general. Individual work also explored how the starvation maintained the parts of her that were afraid to grow up and afraid to stop protecting her parents. We find that keeping a journal makes a client face the extreme nature of their relationship to food without our having to confront them directly. Usually, once they face this relationship themselves their commitment to change increases.

As the issues of denial, dependence, and protection emerged, we explored how these related to her beliefs about men and women in general, and how the anorexia maintained these stereotypic beliefs. We are often amazed to find how much thinking clients have already done on these issues at some level. Janet, like many women who have eating disorders, had parts of her that desperately wanted to grow as an independent woman but felt trapped by loyalties to those around her who held rigidly traditional views about women and men. Anorexia was one way that she avoided facing such conflicts and therapy became a forum for discussing such issues without fearing reproach.

Thus, while Janet began to express her desire for change in her eating and family, we maintained the position that it was equally important to thoroughly explore the potentially negative consequences to these changes. What might she or her family have to give up or acknowledge if she ate normally, and otherwise began to function competently? The following dialogue from a session with Janet illustrates her predicament:

*Therapist*: What would happen if you began to eat regularly and look and feel better?

*Janet*: It would be too scary. I would have to face everything and it is just too much to face. I would have to decide about schools, about a career, about men, about my family, it is all too much. Plus I know I would get fat.

*Therapist*: How do you know that?

*Janet*: This is the thing I have been best at in my life. No one in my family can do this. I would lose control if I started to eat.

As she became increasingly aware of all the areas in her life that anorexia helped her avoid, she began to take the lead in family and sibling session discussions of what they all thought they were avoiding and how they were avoiding these dilemmas. She believed that to be loyal to her mother she should concentrate on having a family and forget about her career. On the other hand, she thought that if she did not go into law or business, she would be unfaithful to her father. Since she believed that a good woman's job is to please others she was in a bind; if she obeyed either injunction she would disappoint someone. In addition, she found both of the alternatives unappealing. The anorexia was her solution to this bind in that it allowed her not to decide on a direction in her life. She could stay close to her mother and help her mother serve others when she was home, while struggling to please her father by going to school but having an excuse for failing. Even her excuse for failing was ostensibly related to another of her parents injunctions to her, which was to be thin and in control of one's appetite. In addition, anorexia allowed her to put off making a career choice, as well as postponing getting involved with a man, since she was asexually thin.

In individual sessions, Janet related how anorexia also provided a way to get nurturant attention and closeness especially from her father but in a way that maintained a certain safe distance and control. She believed that he had always loved his daughters more than his wife and, while she was very uncomfortable about being in that position, parts of her liked the idea that she was so special to him. The anorexia gave her an excuse to express to him and the other members of her family feelings that no one in the family was permitted to express directly – anger and rebelliousness, as well as weakness and neediness.

### Challenging Patterns and Expanding Alternatives

The first several months of treatment were spent defining the issues outlined above and restraining Janet from acting on any of them until she and her family felt ready to handle the consequences of such actions. Those sessions were in preparation for a second stage of treatment during which we challenge the client and her family to address the themes directly and to change the way they interact with each other in the process. The following are conversations excerpted from several different family sessions during this stage. Janet and the therapist spent individual sessions preparing for these family sessions in which she was to make her family see and hear her in a different way. Because of the relatively overt alliance that develops between the client and therapist at this point it is important to have had a number of family sessions during which a strong relationship can be built between the therapist and the other family members.

> *Janet*: (to father) I need more respect from you. I need to know that you think that I am intelligent and not just pretty. (crying) I don't like it when you walk in a room and give me one of your smiles and tell me you wish I was your date. That feels inappropriate. I am a person, I know I am pretty but that is not going to get me anywhere that I want to go. I need your support of me as a competent person.

> *Father*: Most girls think it is neat when their father thinks that they are pretty. I think sometimes you have a way of taking compliments the wrong way. And in the area of intellect, if I did not think you were smart I would have never encouraged you to go to law school.

> *Janet*: I need to be encouraged to be me not to be only what you want me to be "a pretty lawyer."

> *Father*: But we know that is what you could do best. And how much money could you make in Art History?

> Later in the session:
> *Janet*: Can we agree that the next time you come to Chicago that we can try to talk about my life, not only about how I look and how much money I have made? I want you to know me as a person. Can we try?

> *Father*: Sure we can try, but it always seems that you and your mother are too busy to talk to me.

> *Janet*: Dad! Can we try?

During another family session, Janet attempts to create some distance between her and her mother.

> *Janet*: Mom, I know things have never been good for you at home. You never have had anyone to care for you except me

and Lisa (Janet's sister) and we always know when you are unhappy. But I have to know less. You need to change your life. You need to decide about your marriage, get friends, and find someone else to talk to.

*Therapist*: Janet, you need to talk about yourself. If you are asking your mother to depend on you less then you cannot tell her how to run her life. Those are two different messages. Anyway, your parents have been married (turning to the parents) how long?

*Father*: A mighty long time.

*Mother*: Twenty-seven years.

*Therapist*: Twenty-seven years, you can no longer have the power to tell them how to live or to decide about their marriage. Even if they have given that power to you in the past, you can no longer have it, if you are to get on with your life. They have chosen to be married this way, and you cannot tell them to go off in the sunset and be passionately in love or to dump each other. They now must make their own choices. Talk about what you need, as an adult, not as a worry wart.

*Janet*: I need to find a best friend my own age, someone who is experiencing what I am experiencing now. I need to talk to you less and worry about how you are doing less. I guess I need to hear less and also stop initiating conversations about your marriage and your sadness. I want to be close, just not so close, a different close.

*Mother*: (Sits silently crying)

*Therapist*: It must feel like quite a loss to you to hear this?

*Mother*: I never meant to do this to you. I never realized how it affected you.

*Janet*: That does not matter now, I want us to be different, maybe it is just more mature.

Her sessions with her siblings centered on Janet's attempt to join them in their generation. She established peer relationships with them which she never really had. This necessitated created boundaries between the siblings and the parents. She wanted to see them through her eyes not through the eyes of her parents.

The individual sessions concentrated on her own internal conflict resolution between her struggling parts. We worked on her decisions about school, career, and how she wanted to interact with men. Outside of sessions she would take risks in these areas in her life, and make independent decisions based on her own thoughts and feelings, whenever possible. Stage two lasted approximately six months with weekly sessions.

## Consolidation

We knew the consolidation phase was beginning when Janet no longer used therapy to process her life with her friends, family, and work. Rather she used the sessions to report the changes she was making, the risks she was taking, and how she was viewing life differently.

We spent the next few months helping Janet look into her crystal ball and predict areas that might present problems to her. For example, she pretended for a week that she had made the decision to go study in Europe. During the week she tried to imagine her fears and how she would cope, the conversations she would have with people regarding this decision, and then actually preparing to leave. We went through each of these practice situations focusing on career, lovers, friends, and family.

We also discussed how to use therapy and our relationship in the future; to keep the options open and see therapy as preventive from now on, not only for crisis. To ignore the message she previously believed, which was that women feel their feelings too much and that feelings are a sign of weakness and therapy is a sign of weakness.

With her family, we cemented many of the changed relationships and talked about what all the members had contributed to the successful changes. We also explored potential pitfalls. Can the kids stay out of the marriage? Can the parents allow the kids to make their own career decisions? Can the family members have the freedom to make their own definitions of man and woman?

Janet called almost two years after her last session. She had moved to go to art school in New York and called because she was leaving to go to Italy to study Art History. She was scared and wanted to talk. We discussed all her wonderful changes since we had last met, change in her major in school, in her family's support of that change, how the risk of Europe scared her, excited her but did not immobilize her. As she left she said to me something that summarizes the dilemma of many of the women we treat with eating disorders. She said:

> You know I never really wanted to die back then, I didn't want to be dead, I just didn't want to be alive. Living was so confusing and so hard, and I had no idea what it meant to be a woman and a person, I just wanted to stand still, not dead, just not living.

## SUMMARY

This paper highlighted the interdependent nature of society, family, and self with respect to women and the eating disorders of bulimia and anorexia nervosa. These eating disorders are perplexing and frightening symptoms that cannot be understood or treated without examining and emphasizing the role of women, in all contexts. When these roles change then the need for these eating disorders will no longer exist.

## REFERENCES

Bennett, W. & Gavin, J. (1982). *The Dieter's Dilemma*. New York: Basic Books.

Boskin-Lodahl, M. (1986). Cinderella's stepsisters: A feminist perspective on anorexia nervosa and bulimia. *Signs: Journal of Women in Culture and Society*, 2, 342-356.

Boskin-White, M. & White, W.C. (1983). *Bulimarexia: The Binge/Purge Cycle*. New York: Norton & Co.

Bruch, H. (1973) *Eating Disorders: Obesity, Anorexia Nervosa and the Person*. New York: Basic Books.

Casper, R. (1983). On the emergence of bulimia nervosa as a syndrome. *International Journal of Eating Disorders*, 2, 3-16.

Dwyer, J. T., Feldman, J.J., Seltzer, C.C. & Mayer, J. (1969). Adolescent attitudes toward weight and appearance. *Journal of Nutrition Education*, 1, 14-19.

Fisch, R., Weakland, J. & Segal, L. (1982). *The Tactics of Change*. San Francisco: Jossey-Bass.

Garfinkel, P. E. & Garner, D.M. (1982). *Anorexia Nervosa: A Multidimensional Perspective*. New York: Brunner/Mazel.

Garner, D.M., Garfinkel, P.E., Schwartz, D. & Thompson, M. (1980). Cultural expectations of thinness in women. *Psychological Reports*, 47, 483-491.

Haley, J. (1976). *Problem Solving Therapy*. San Francisco: Jossey-Bass.

Henry, J. (1963). *Culture Against Man*. New York: Random House.

Hueneman, R.L., Shapiro, L.R., Hampton, M. C. & Mitchell, B.W. (1986). A longitudinal study of gross body composition and body conformation and their association with food and activity in a teen population. *American Journal of Clinical Nutrition*, 18, 325-338.

Jakobovits, C., Hatstead, D., Kelly, L., Roe, D. & Young, C.M. (1977). Eating habits and nutrient intakes of college women over a thirty year period. *Journal of American Dietetic Association*, 71, 405-411.

Madanes, C. (1984). *Strategic Family Therapy*. San Francisco: Jossey-Bass.

Menzies, I.E.P. (1970). Psychosocial aspects of eating. *Journal of Psychosomatic Research*, 14, 223-227.

Minuchin, S. & Fishman, H.C. (1981). *Family Therapy Techniques*. Cambridge, MA: Harvard University Press.

Minuchin, S., Rosman, B. & Baker, L. (1978). *Psychosomatic Families: Anorexia Nervosa in Context*. Cambridge, MA: Harvard University Press.

Orbach, S. (1978). *Fat is a Feminist Issue*. London: Paddington Press.

Polivy, J. & Herman, P. (1983). *Breaking the Diet Habit*. New York: Basic Books.

Schwartz, R.C. (1986). Intrapsychic processed revisited: A systemic model of internal family therapy. Unpublished manuscript.

Schwartz, R.C., Barrett, M.J. & Saba, G. (1985). Family therapy for bulimia. In D. Garner & P. Garfinkel (Eds.), *Handbook for Psychotherapy for Anorexia Nervosa and Bulimia*. New York: Guilford.

Schwartz, R.C., Barrett, M.J. & Saba, G. (in press). *The Systemic Treatment of the Bulimic Family and Individual*. New York: Guilford.

Wooley, S.C. & Wooley, O.W. (1980). Eating disorders: Obesity and anorexia. In R.T. Hare-Mustin & A.M. Brodsky (Eds.), *Women and Psychotherapy*. New York; Guilford Press.

Wyden, P. (1965). *The Overweight Society*. New York: Morrow.

# Women, Family Therapy, and Larger Systems

## Linda Webb-Watson (Woodard)

**SUMMARY.** Feminist critique of family therapy has articulated many of the issues that are relevant to working with women and their families. An examination of the ways in which family therapists may unintentionally support the sexist notions of the larger system and ways to handle these situations so that a transformative experience for the larger system may begin is offered.

It's mostly my fault because I work too much. When I come home, I'm tired and don't get things done.

They said at school that John's problem is that he doesn't have a father or male figure to relate to. They suggested that I call "Big Brothers" and put him on the waiting list. But what do I do until he gets a "Big Brother?"

These or similar statements are heard in almost every therapist's office who works with women and children and serve to highlight the questions posed by this paper: Are the statements above contagious? What can a family therapist do to stop the spread of the germs? Or, to pose it differently: In what ways do I, as a family therapist, perpetuate these notions in my practice? If one considers the numbers of women from diverse backgrounds who make similar statements, one might be in awe of the magnitude of the coincidence. Overlay the sociopolitical context and coincidence disappears. This paper is written to encourage a personal examination of the ways in which we participate in perpetuating ideas that are not helpful to ourselves or to our clients. Exploration of work with the

Linda Webb-Watson (Woodard), EdD, is affiliated with Salesmanship Club Youth and Family Centers, Inc., 3505 Turtle Creek Boulevard, Suite 114, Dallas, TX 75219.

*145*

larger systems in which families find themselves is offered as a beginning.

The feminist critique of psychotherapy and, more recently, of family therapy has described the issues that women face both as therapists and as clients (Ault-Riché, 1986; Brodsky & Hare-Mustin, 1980; Chesler, 1972; Hare-Mustin, 1978; Libow, 1986; Taggart, 1985). One aspect of the critique is an insistence on analyses that do not accept traditional ideas of psychological development based primarily on male development. An understanding of how symptom presentation is impacted by biological changes within the female life cycle is also mandatory for appropriate nonsexist intervention. In addition, the place of women in the context of their families, and in light of larger system expectations, has been pointed to as significant.

The family as a conservative institution, socializes its members to accept the role assignments which are supported by the society as a whole. Family therapy can unwittingly cooperate in the maintenance and support of outmoded gender distinctions when therapists fail to recognize the influence of the economic, social, and political system, on the individual and her family (James & McIntyre, 1983; Taggart, 1985). Particularly important, and yet extremely elusive, is how the powerful systems of society coerce family structure to be what it is. This coercion includes not only what is considered "family" but also the definition and operation of the roles, relationships, and expectations of those participating in it. As Taggart (1985) states " . . . the boundary between 'family' and the broad social context which defines it has become a *barrier* that prevents exploration of connectedness between them" (p. 116).

It is interesting that this issue continuously emerges in feminist critiques since one of the major contributions of family therapy has been the appreciation for contextual variables as they influence human behavior. While the heritage of family therapy has encouraged therapists to examine these contextual variables and lip service is given to this activity, too often, in the privacy of our practices we opt for what is comfortable, easy, and not too time consuming. The appreciation, for the particular socio-political context in which families (or individual family members) "have" their problem is avoided for what seems to be the more manageable, immediate, and apparent situation. In this sense the boundary that Taggart refers to emerges out of a need to economize time and energy. It is a shorthand that has its utility but like other shorthand methods, it can lose richness and rigidify in definition over time. For example, think of the development of the shorthand phrase "women and other minorities." This shorthand evolved, in part, as difficulties were encountered with addressing the impact of class and culture on women's issues. "Women" became a further shorthand for "white women." The shorthand perhaps has utility but it has also robbed all women of the richness and diversity of our own collective experience and supports a certain sociopolitical reality between white women and women of color. In a similar way our shorthand, "family" as a system separate from other systems, supports a certain reality which significantly narrows pathways of change.

In light of these issues, it is appropriate that attention shifts to the multiple levels at which a woman's existence is defined. Failure to see women and their families in the sociopolitical context in which they exist is the same barrier which inhibits therapists from examining the political nature of therapy. That is, the action of diagnosing and intervening with clients has a political reality as well as a therapeutic reality. Rather than labeling therapy as interactive with an ongoing political process, Edelman (1974) suggests that ". . . psychiatrists reinforce the norm that cheerful adjustment to poverty or war is healthy while despondency or anger in the face of these pathologies is sick; but their decisions are labelled 'medical'" (p. 22). To address the interactive nature of therapy with the political process, an understanding of larger systems and their effect on ourselves and our clients is relevant.

When therapists work with larger systems there are usually at least two levels of intervention that are evident most of the time. The first is the level on which changes in policy are required. In most large systems a significant length of time is needed for policy change to occur. Most often addressing this level takes political or legal action. The second level of intervention is the alleviation of the immediate problem-maintaining relationship for the family. While it is not the intention to minimize the necessity for change in social policy, this paper focuses on those problem-maintaining relationships and our role in perpetuating them.

## EVOLUTION OF WORKING WITH LARGER SYSTEMS

The thinking about larger systems interfaces is not new. Minuchin et al. (1967) addressed the impact of the ecological context of families living in poverty. Aponte (1976) and Tucker and Dyson

(1976) explored the interface of schools and families. Haley (1976) cautioned therapists about the possibilities for social control. Selvini Palazzoli et al. (1980a) discussed the significance of the referring person to the understanding of the problem system. As these works contributed to the evolution of work with families and larger systems, several authors (Imber-Black, 1983a, 1983b, 1986; Miller, 1983; Webb-Watson & Woodard, 1983) articulated their notions about the dilemmas of the family-larger system interface. While the focus of attention was the larger system's place in problem maintenance, it was also noticed that while change in the family was facilitated that same change facilitated stability in the larger system. Imber-Black (1983c) pointed to the place of family therapy in the homeostasis of larger systems. The illustrations that follow illuminate our often unwitting participation in larger system stability.

Single parent women, in the first therapy interview, often indicate that part of the problem is that the children don't have a father. They appear hopeless, at their wits' end, and unable to implement anything that might work. These women have become convinced of their incompetence by the continuous messages they receive in the media, schools, and churches, at work, from psychologists/therapists, from other women, and from men.

There are several ways in which family therapists can inadvertently highlight this point of view for the women. For instance, male therapists may get a referral because "the adolescent male needs a male image." This request may come from a mother directly or from other referral sources. In either case, she now has a man who can "fix things." To avoid providing verification of the larger system point of view, the therapist should include the problem system in the initial interviews. If a mother is the source of referral, he should encourage her toward self-determination, highlighting her competence and ability to handle the situation. In addition, he must avoid appearing to have an "inside track" with male children by deferring to mother's expertise with them. For example, a male therapist on a family therapy team received a self referral from a mother who wanted the therapist to talk to her son man-to-man. The therapist deferred to the mother, and the team sent in supportive messages to her always beginning with the phrase, "The women on the team. . . ." Fortunately the therapist had no children so he could easily defer to her knowledge and continue with a one-down position. Over the course of a few sessions, the mother became much more confident in her ability to manage her son.

Women more frequently are the focus of treatment (Imber-Black, 1986) and as such are often offered multiple services. Family therapists who refer or who accept referrals of women as part of a multiple system treatment process highlight the assumptions that women are most often the ones who need to be changed as well as the ones who are less competent to handle their problems. As a family therapist who thinks in terms of her place in the larger system, careful consideration should be given to multiple referrals which introduce the women to artificial helping/support systems rather than build her own natural supports. In the event that the family therapist is part of a larger system treatment plan, utilizing the notion of the problem system and holding meetings of those participants is probably the most useful direction in which to proceed. The intent is to interrupt the reason for the referral which implicitly challenges the assumptions of the larger system and opens up other avenues for exploration.

For the author, the early years were marked by ideas that were consistent with what is sometimes termed the "old" epistemology: the symptom creates the problem. Having come into family therapy after years of political activism, it was easy to accept that systems were discreet, hierarchically ordered entities, with each level of the system being responsible for the next largest unit until one reached THE SYSTEM (meaning society's institution) which was responsible for the oppression of us all. It seemed reasonable that if one hypothesized that marital conflict supported the child's symptoms in a family, one could also hypothesize that sexism (for example) in society supported certain types of marital conflicts in couples. From this point of view when an African-American child had a school problem, one could assume that the school system was responsible. The therapist's direction was clear and certain interventions became obvious. Since this stance, which would usually lead to confrontation, had varying degrees of success/failure, ideas of what might work better had to emerge.

Hoffman (1985) identified the "new" epistemology which "implies that the problem creates the system" (p. 386) and which summarized, in different ways, emergence of thinking about system interfaces. Using the same example from this point of view, the school problem of the African-American child organized many people into a system. They exchanged and created the meanings surrounding the problem. As Hoffman further suggested, "The problem is the meaning system created by the distress and the treatment unit is everyone who is contributing to that meaning system" (p. 387). And if we saw ourselves as a part of the systems (Von Foerster, 1981) in which we worked we would be better able to comprehend how we might be supporting the very thing we hope to change.

The most recent step in the evolution of the work with larger systems has been an appreciation for the recursiveness of the two ideas outlined above. The "old" epistemology allows for critique, goal setting, and direction. The "new" epistemology increases the number of vehicles one has to achieve the goal.

Specific ideas and techniques that appear in the family therapy literature apply to the work with family-larger systems (Fisch, Weakland & Segal, 1982; Minuchin & Fishman, 1981; Selvini-Palazzoli, Boscolo, Cecchin & Prata, 1980b) and are used to guide the therapist's decision and choice of stance.


## ASSESSMENT

From the map offered above one can assume that with referrals from larger systems, that referring systems becomes part of the unit of treatment and they are included in the treatment in appropriate ways. Naturally, this means that the therapist must be willing to hold sessions in places other than her office.

For obvious reasons, the most maneuverable position for the therapist is the nonjudgmental or neutral stance (Fisch, Weakland & Segal, 1982; Selvini-Palazzoli, Boscolo, Cecchin & Prata, 1980b). This is the stance that is chosen as a starting point for treatment. The therapist is able to freely interact with the participants of the "problem system" without engendering defensiveness on their part. The implication of this stance is an abandonment of the pursuit of blame or fault, substituting that activity with the pursuit of discovering new openings for understanding the distress.

Several aspects are significant in the assessment process. When working with a problem system the therapist is aware that those participants from larger systems are merely representatives of that system and not the system itself. It is helpful to understand, at least to a limited extent, the context in which that person must work. For example, in working with a child protective agency it is useful to know how that agency is organized. In addition, a sense of the relationship between the caseworker and her supervisor may be useful to your assessment.

Discerning the disagreements among the helpers and/or disagreements between helpers and family members can lead to hypotheses regarding problem maintenance. Questioning would include both who disagrees with whom about what and how that disagreement is acted out in the problem system. Circular questioning provides one of the most efficient tools for assessing and intervening in this regard. It can be used to determine the fixed beliefs of the participants in the problem system. Often we have found it is through the management of meaning (either through reframing and/or positive connotation) that openings are "discovered" in the distress.

Other information that may be useful in comprehending the problem system is gained through a structural assessment which delineates coalition and splits and an examination of the attempted solutions that have been employed over time.

## HYPOTHESIZING

Hypothesizing plays a significant role in this work. An hypothesis is a descriptive device that possesses at least three elements. The first is that the hypothesis is primarily useful rather than primarily truthful. This allows for the abandonment of a search for the truth and facilitates the development of description upon which action can be taken. The second element is a recognition that a hypothesis emerges as a particular point of view at a particular point in time. What this means is that a hypothesis is subject to change as time and circumstances move on. Finally, the systemic hypothesis is an attempt to link a description of symptomatic behavior to the various members within the interacting systems.

## TREATMENT PLANNING AND INTERVENTIONS

Assessment and hypothesizing lead to treatment planning and intervention. Planning is a significant aspect of treatment and plans usually directly flow from the hypotheses that are generated. Further, the hypotheses that are developed help the therapist to decide which stance(s) she will take during the course of therapy. Aside from the neutral stance, we sometimes must take another stance with larger systems. We term it the advocacy stance and in our work it usually means some fairly active, goal-directed interventions in order to encourage the larger systems to behave in a different way with the family. The therapist maintains her nonblame position but has a clear agenda to be accomplished. The advocacy stance arises when the primary punctuation is on the premise: the system created the problem.

For example, in Texas the law requires that schools offer tutoring to any child who is failing a class. For some schools this law is not followed. To take an advocacy stance is to insist that the child be offered the tutoring or a reasonable alternative. Perhaps, in this case, confrontation is the appropriate intervention.

The stance at any particular point in the treatment generates interventions that are consistent with it. The therapist can delineate boundaries and specify roles so that the family can determine the amount and type of contact needed. Reframing (e.g., from adversaries to partners working together) and then facilitating a structuring of the relationship is often effective. Circular questioning leading to a systemic opinion can also be used in intervening with multiple helpers. These interventions often clear the way for resolution of the presenting problem and generate new information about previously held assumptions.

The following case illustrates both race and sex assumptions and the handling of it from a larger system perspective.

Adrienne Green, a 9-year-old African-American child and her mother were referred by a private school. Ms. Green was a single parent and earned less than $9,000 per year as a day care teacher. The school had very few African-American children and a good percentage of those in attendance were on a scholarship program that the school had established. The reason for the referral was that Adrienne was being verbally and physically aggressive in class. Her teacher was sending notes home daily indicating everything that Adrienne did wrong for the day. Ms. Green desperately wanted her daughter to achieve at this school because she viewed it as a great opportunity for her daughter to eventually get out of poverty. The initial interview revealed Adrienne to be an outspoken, assertive child. She indicated that she "didn't take any mess" from the children at school and that the teacher picked on her. Ms. Green appeared torn between wanting to support her daughter and wanting her to blend in at school. Ms. Green indicated that she did not have any significant complaints about the child's behavior at home.

This case could have been handled so that it was homeostatic for the larger system. Myths supported by the larger system that were implied in the referral included: (1) African-American children are aggressive and are in need of being controlled; (2) single parent African-American households are pathologic and require intensive intervention to correct defects; (3) the problem in education today is the lack of motivation on the part of the children and the lack of parental involvement and interest; and (4) little girls should never be aggressive and independent.

It would have been possible to begin working with this family from any of the operating premises listed above. Accepting the referral from the school without asking questions about the meaning system between the family and the school would have been an implicit verification of the accuracy of the referral. Whatever reasons the teacher had for referring the child would be validated and she would likely become more convinced of the truth of her observation.

Acceptance of the referral as it was made would also have had specific influence on the course of treatment. Depending upon the model of therapy, attempts might have been made to teach Ms. Green more effective parenting skills or encourage Adrienne to express "appropriately" rather than "act-out" her feeling. The investigation could have led to finding a problem in the family's hierarchy. A hypothesis could have been generated that perhaps there was a grandmother who was undermining mother's authority or that the child's problem served a protective function for her mother. This is not to suggest that these interventions might not also have "worked."

Adrienne's "school problem" could have been cured and the referring system could maintain its beliefs about African-American and single parent families. However, some of us want to influence larger systems to handle people in more expansive ways and take these opportunities to do just that.

When the problem system is taken into account different questions are posed which alter the course of treatment. The first family-school interview revealed a cycle of blame and counterblame between the parent and the teacher. The principal and school counselor argued with the teacher that Adrienne had problems. The school counselor felt that perhaps Adrienne should be moved to a classroom with a male teacher. Many of the disagreements centered around differences in expectations and styles of approaching certain situations. With no ill intention, the school had an investment in seeing African-Americans as having problems which could be ameliorated through the academic program and/or a psychological referral. From their point of view, they admitted these children as a contribution to an improved social order.

A classroom observation was scheduled. Observation of the child within the context of the classroom supported a hypothesis that cultural differences in behavior and expectations were part of the problem. Adrienne was the only African-American child in the classroom. The teacher focused a significant amount of her attention on the child, highlighting, through that attention, the "differentness" between this child and the others. There were some specific points of conflict identified by the teacher. She cited the child's failure to use eye contact, a sign which indicated dishonesty to the teacher. She was also concerned about Adrienne's unwillingness to take directions from the other children, suggesting that Adrienne was too independent.

The teacher seemed genuinely concerned about Adrienne so it was assumed that she would respond to an educative intervention which addressed the manifestations of cultural conflict in the classroom along with specific information regarding African-American child rearing practices (Abrahams & Troike, 1972). By informing her about these differences, we began reframing the child's behavior as "cultural" rather than "bad." This relieved the teacher of the responsibility she felt for taking some kind of corrective actions. She began to understand the behavior as normal for this child. Consultation sessions with the teacher and school counselor highlighted the strengths that Adrienne brought to the classroom.

To the family the problem was also reframed as a cultural conflict in which everyone was having difficulty in making effective transitions from one culture to another. Ms. Green and her daughter worked together on translations from home culture to school culture. In this way, there was simultaneous support for Ms. Green's desire to side with her daughter and make it in school.

Another family-school interview was conducted with the intention of establishing a relationship characterized by "working together" on the problem of translations. A great deal of excitement was generated at the school because there now was an alternative explanation for some of the problems they had identified with African-American children. From our point of view, the therapy created a workable reality in which the problems could be addressed. Adrienne is doing well in school and is seen as different in a new way which validates her life experiences and values. Parenthetically, the teacher confided that she was impressed with how convinced she was of Ms. Green's strength and capability.

## CONCLUSION

The vision of work with larger systems requires continuous expansion. As we reflect on the ways in which the act of family therapy is part of the politics of our society, greater clarity will be gained on our role in the stability and change of larger systems particularly as it relates to the issues of gender, culture, and class. An apparently useful direction is the continued elaboration of the family therapist's part in the problem system. More detailed examples of creating contexts for change when multiple systems are involved should provide us with openings to examine all of this in different lights.

## REFERENCES

Abrahams, R. D. & Troike, R. C. (Eds.). (1972). *Language and cultural diversity in American education*. Englewood Cliffs, NJ: Prentice Hall, Inc.

Aponte, H. (1976). The family-school interview: An ecostructural approach. *Family Process, 15*, 303-311.

Ault-Riché, M. (1986). A feminist critique of five schools of family therapy. In M. Ault-Riché (Ed.), *Women and family therapy*. Rockville, MD: Aspen Systems Corporation, 1986.

Brodsky, A. M. & Hare-Mustin, R. T. (Eds.). (1980). *Women and psychotherapy*. New York: Guilford.

Chesler, P. (1972). *Women and madness*. New York: Doubleday.

Edelman, M. (1974). *Language and social problems*. Institute For Research on Poverty Discussion Papers. Madison, WI: University of Wisconsin.

Fisch, R., Weakland, J. H. & Segal, L. (1982). *The tactics of change*. San Francisco, CA: Jossey-Bass Publishers.

Haley, J. (1976). *Problem solving therapy*. San Francisco, CA: Jossey-Bass.

Hare-Mustin, R. T. (1978). A feminist approach to family therapy. *Family Process, 17*, 181-193.

Hoffman, L. (1985). Beyond power and control: Toward a "second order" family systems therapy. *Family Systems Medicine, 3*, 381-396.

Imber-Black (Coppersmith), E. (1983a). The family and public sector systems: Interviewing and interventions. *Journal of Strategic and Systemic Therapies, 2*, 38-47.

Imber-Black (Coppersmith). E. (1983b). The family and public service systems: An assessment method. In B. Kenney (Ed.). *Diagnosis and assessment in family therapy*. Rockville, MD: Aspen Systems Corporation.

Imber-Black (Coppersmith), E. (1983c). The place of family therapy in the homeostasis of larger systems. In M. Aronson & R. Wolberg (Eds.), *Group and family therapy: An overview*. New York: Bruner/Mazel.

Imber-Black (Coppersmith), E. (1984). The systemic consultant and human service provider systems. In L. Wynne (Ed.). *Family therapist as consultant*, New York: Guilford Press.

Imber-Black (Coppersmith), E. (1986). Women, families and larger systems. In M. Ault-Riché (Ed.), *Women and family therapy*. Rockville, MD: Aspen Systems Corporation.

Jackson, D. D. (1957). The question of family homeostasis. *Psychiatric Quarterly. Supplement, 31*, 79-90.

James, K. & McIntyre, D. (1983). The reproduction of families: The social role of family therapy. *Journal of Marital and Family Therapy, 9*, 119-129.

Libow, J. A. (1986). Training family therapists as feminists. In M. Ault-Riché (Ed.), *Women and family therapy*. Rockville, MD: Aspen Systems Corporation.

Miller, D. (1983). Outlaws and invaders: The adaptive function of alcohol abuse in the family-helper supra system. *Journal of Strategic and Systemic Therapies, 2*, 15-27.

Minuchin, S. & Fishman, H. C. (1981). *Family therapy techniques*. Cambridge, MA: Harvard University Press.

Minuchin, S., Montalvo, B., Guerney, B., Rosman, B. & Shumer, F. (1967). *Families of the slums: An exploration of their structure and treatment*. New York: Basic Books.

Selvini-Palazzoli, M., Boscolo, L., Cecchin, G. & Prata, J. (1980a). The problem of the referring person. *Journal of Marital and Family Therapy, 6*, 3-9.

Selvini-Palazzoli, M., Boscolo, L., Cecchin, G. & Prata, J. (1980b). Hypothesizing, circularity, neutrality: Three guidelines for the conductor of the session. *Family Process, 19*, 3-12.

Taggart, M. (1985). The feminist critique in epistemological perspective: Questions of context in family therapy. *Journal of Marital and Family Therapy, 11*. 113-126.

Tucker, B. Z. & Dyson, E. (1976). The family and the school: Utilizing human resources to promote learning. *Family Process, 15*, 125-141.

Von Foerster, H. (1981). *Observing systems*. Seaside, CA: Intersystems Publications.

Webb-Woodard, L. & Woodard, B. (1983). The larger system in the treatment of incest. *Journal of Strategic and Systemic Therapies, 2*, 28-37.

# Women, Rituals,
# and Family Therapy

Joan Laird
Ann Hartman

**SUMMARY.** The function and power of rituals are explored as they express and define women's status, roles, and relationships. The ritual life of contemporary American women is described and the need to alter, enrich, and develop new rituals more expressive of the tasks and transitions faced by women today is argued. The relationship between ritual and therapy is developed as it is demonstrated that ritual can be mobilized as a powerful instrument in therapy. Examples from practice illustrate that women, in family of origin work and in conjoint family therapy, can be helped to challenge and reshape their ritual lives.

Ritual is one of the most powerful socialization mechanisms known. Through our daily rituals, our domestic and public ceremonies, our rites of passage which accompany birth, marriage, death, and the other important markers of our lives, we define and reaffirm our traditions and ourselves. While words may accompany ritual, ritual takes us beyond language and beyond our conscious, cognitive categories, because of its powerful use of myth, metaphor, and symbol. Above all, however, ritual implies action. It is performed, enacted, reflecting the past and shaping the future at one and the same time.

This article explores the issue of women and ritual, seeking a beginning answer to the questions: (1) What rituals are available for women in our society? (2) What are the form and content of our public and domestic rituals as they affect women? (3) What are their implications for women's lives and for women's self-definitions?

Joan Laird, MS, ACSW, is Adjunct Associate Professor, Boston University School of Social Work and private practice. Ann Hartman, DSW, ACSW, is Dean, Smith College School for Social Work. Address correspondence to Joan Laird, 15 Frost Lane, Hadley MA 01035.

and (4) How and in what ways can the power of ritual be marshalled for change in therapy with women and families? We begin with an overview of the concept of "ritual" through a brief exploration of its definitions and functions. This material is followed by an examination of American cultural rituals, both domestic and public, as they facilitate or hinder woman's development over the life cycle and her participation in family life. We then discuss the relationship between ritual and family therapy, exploring how the power of ritual can be mobilized in therapy and how women can be helped to claim and reshape their own rituals.

## RITUAL: AN OVERVIEW

Ritual has been defined as "the basic social act" by Rappoport (1979), who sees the form of ritual as the source of its power. Others have defined ritual largely in terms of its functions, that is, in terms of what may be accomplished in and through ritual. There is, however, a great deal of debate in the anthropological literature over the issue of whether ritual should be considered a force for order, balance, homeostasis, an essentially preserving mechanism, or whether ritual can also be disordering, unbalancing, and disintegrative. Most agree, however, that rituals always include repetition, performance, special behavior or stylization, order, evocative presentational style, and a collective dimension (that is, a dimension charged with a social message, even if it is the self sending a message to self). Elements of chaos and spontaneity may appear at particular times and places (Moore and Myerhoff, 1977).

Rituals may be performed individually, as in the morning cleansing of the body, meditation, or aerobics. Rituals are also enacted collectively in small and large gatherings, as in once or rarely performed national "happenings" such as in the recent celebration of the Statue of Liberty or in an intimate celebration of a wedding anniversary. A particular ritual may be largely unique to an individual or family or it may draw heavily on themes, meanings, and symbols available in the larger society (Wolin & Bennett, 1984). In Friedman's (1980) view, it is the family that selects from the larger culture what rituals it wishes to incorporate, and it is the family which determines the emotional quality and thus the success of a particular ritual. Rituals also vary greatly in the extent to which they hold room for spontaneity, creativity, and flexibility or bind us to rigid and repetitive actions which have lost their old meanings in new contexts. And, since rituals may be enacted without critical, conscious awareness, they may reinforce prescriptions for behavior and self-concepts which are dissonant with the times or with personal choices and may be individually stultifying.

Through ritual we learn who we are to be and how we are to act, as members of a particular culture, subculture, and family. Social rituals don't just express our realities, they help create them. Families develop their own unique cultures over the generations. In a family, as in a small society, those fundamental and enduring assumptions that constitute the family's culture, its shared world view or paradigm, are thought to be reinforced and transmitted intergenerationally through ritual (Reiss, 1981). As particular prescriptions for behavior and moral stances are enacted in ritual, our social roles are expressed and shaped. Thus order is brought to our lives, and the chaos of potential choices brought under control. Rituals not only bring order, however; they also enable, announce, and impose change (Myerhoff, 1983). Furthermore, rituals often contain paradoxical elements, presenting us with opposite truths and minimizing or disguising differences, inequities, or injustices. Because rituals are enacted, taking us beyond conscious levels of awareness, they can simultaneously command our attention and loyalty and deflect our questioning. In this case, doing is believing or, as Kenneth Burke has said, "Ritual is dancing an attitude" (Burke, as quoted by Myerhoff [1983]).

## WOMEN AND RITUAL

Very little is known about women's rituals; they are understudied. Until recently, anthropologists, who in addition to theologians and psychiatrists, serve as our primary ritual scholars and specialists, had virtually ignored women's lives. What is known of women's lives in most societies has been based largely on the male anthropologist's interpretation of the male informant's interpretation of the worlds of women.

Second, women's rituals everywhere tend to be allocated to the domestic sphere, men's to the public or community. That is, those rituals that do exist for women tend to express, celebrate, and reinforce woman's role as nurturer and caretaker and her assignment, whether she is child, wife, or mother, to a particular lineage and to a particular male. Puberty rites for girls, for example, ready them for sexual relationships with and service to men, as well as preparation for domestic life. In our own society, in the traditional marriage ceremony women are *given* away by their fathers to grooms they promise to obey. While this symbolism has lost some of its original meaning, in many societies women still are considered properties which are transferred between lineages.[1]

Gluck, Dannefer, and Milea (1980) have pointed out that women tend to structure their lives (and, we would add, their rituals) around a range of contingencies that depend on others. These contingencies include:

> the need to fit the expectancies of an unknown spouse, the uncertainty about whether she will marry, and the necessity to provide a backup education and training "just in case" she does not, the possibility of childlessness, with the concomitant need to develop alternative activities, the disruption of routine when the children leave home, with the concomitant need to develop other options, and the possibility of divorce or widowhood, with the resulting necessity to prepare for some sort of occupation, again "just in case." (Russo, 1978, p. 114, quoted in Gluck, Dannefer & Milea, 1980, p. 296)

Male rituals, on the other hand, tend to express men's participation in and control of public life; such rituals incorporate values and traditions that construct and reconstruct for males a higher authority in the public world (Bamberger, 1974).

It is only relatively recently that women have participated in equal numbers in college education, one of contemporary society's most powerful markers for movement from the domestic to the public world. While women have been entering fields formerly the exclusive province of men, men still tend to occupy, within these fields, those offices most endowed with ritual power in the expression and definition of social and cultural mores.

A third generalization we may make is that women's rituals not only tend to be less public or important but in most societies fewer rituals exist for women. For example, rite of passage rituals that clearly help females incorporate difficult life transitions by defining and celebrating new statuses are rare. Thus many societies have elaborate puberty rituals for males, while girls' puberty rituals are less common and certainly less elaborate. There are no female counterparts for the elaborate rituals of the largely male military, no colorful or dramatic ways that women may "earn their stripes" as men do in the Army or on the college football team.

A final impression is that even when women's role in ritual is central, as is the case in our own domestic holiday celebrations, it often has more to do with the work and less to do with the honor and glory attached to ritual. In certain parts of Mexico, for example, women toil through the night grinding corn and preparing food to be used in the elaborate and colorful festivals in which the men parade and dance.

## WOMEN'S RITUALS: CHARACTERISTICS AND MESSAGES

What are the characteristics of the major rituals in which women participate? What messages about women and their roles, their relationships to others, are contained in women's rituals? Many of the private and public rituals in which woman engages or is exhorted to engage in have to do with purification, with ritually cleansing her body. In traditional societies, women may remain in special huts during menstruation, or may be isolated from the larger community for several weeks after childbirth, undergoing a number of purification rituals before they are considered ready for reentry, that is, no longer a danger to the community.

A contemporary ritual which contains elements of purification and reaffirms an ideal order of sex roles is of course the Miss America beauty pageant, an annual rite of fall. The contestants parade their clean, shapely, and presumably fecund bodies while a male host notes their forms and barks their accomplishments, an all-male board plans the pageant, and a largely male jury judges the goods, a ritual reminiscent of the slave auctions of the 18th and 19th centuries or the cattle auctions which still take place.

Why must women devote such energy to cleansing and purifying themselves? Women everywhere have been defined as the "other," a marked category in relation to the more generic unmarked category "male." Women, perhaps because they lactate and bleed, are seen as closer to nature than to culture, as unclean, as sexually polluted and polluting (Ortner, 1974). Douglas (1966) has hypothesized that rituals associated with cleanliness and purity reflect and maintain the ordered patterning, the structures which a culture represents and seeks to maintain. Central to such structures and patterns are, of course, the relations between men and women, and thus pollution ideas are enlisted to bind men and women to their allotted roles. Douglas (1966) suggests that in cases where the social system is well-articulated, articulate powers are vested in the points of authority; in such societies purification rituals may be largely unnecessary. Where the social structure is ill-articulated and sex roles, for example, may be highly ambiguous or changing, those who challenge the formerly established order represent disorder, danger, and pollution, and are thus in need of constant and reassuring purification. The polluting person, she suggests, is always in the wrong; she has crossed some invisible line which should not have been crossed, unleashing danger for someone, danger perhaps for an ideology, a system of ideas. Today, in our own society, women are competing for positions of authority, are seeking more power and control over public ritual, are crossing formerly uncrossable lines, and thus may be seen as posing a threat to those reluctant or fearful to share authority. One way of preserving the status quo, then, of guarding the secret symbols, is to use violence, another powerful and deadly strategy is to continue to support and enact public, private, and therapeutic rituals in which certain kinds of roles are reinforced, statuses preserved, and definitional images projected.

Domestic and public rituals order daily events and human interactions and define male-female roles and relationships. Many rituals enact a dominance-submission theme. In many if not most societies, women must in both their public and private lives display deference to men, reinforcing definitions of power and authority. Deference of women toward men may be expressed, for example, in physical positioning. In this society, men generally "top" women, biologically as well as in sexual intercourse or in family photographs. Good manners dictate that a man rises as a woman enters a room. Although ostensibly a mark of deference toward the woman, the effect is that the man is once again "taller," not subjected to a position in which a woman is looking down upon him. Deference of women toward men may be expressed in forms of address, in the topics which may be raised, in the ways males and females enter or leave rooms, in rules which regulate nonverbal motions such as eye contact or ritual nodding or bowing. Female ritual deference is also seen in seating arrangements. For example, the male's head-of-family status is symbolized by his position at the head of the table, while women sit at the foot, or at the feet of, men.

Even in modern holiday celebrations, which Caplow et al. (1982)

believe are designed to honor mother, hearth, and home and to mask the paradoxes inherent in the modern woman's life, women do most of the work, while men's greater authority is recognized in subtle, symbolic ways. Women toil for weeks, for example, preparing for holidays, shopping for food and gifts, cleaning, cooking, and decorating. The male generally presides on these occasions, reminding all assembled that he is the "head of the family." As husband and father, it is usually he who distributes the gifts and who is handed the ceremonial knife in preparation for the ritual carving of the roast or turkey. In former times it was the male who hunted for the meat — perhaps now the ritual carving reminds everyone who it is that has brought home the bacon. Interestingly enough, the presiding task is often so tiring that men must rest while women clean up, again perhaps a survival from an earlier time when men would come home exhausted after the hunt.

In the public world, women play supportive roles in rituals that are designed specifically for men: the taking of the minutes at the corporate board meeting, the ritualized handing over of the surgical instruments as a male doctor helps a woman deliver her baby, cheering on the male athletes and the audience during a contest of skill. Football, as one examines the roles of player and cheerleader, the costumes, and the behaviors, provides a dramatic illustration of how male and female cultural definitions are expressed and reinforced in contemporary ritual.

Finally, both paucity and contingency characterize woman's ritual life over her life cycle. Most of the transitions in the woman's life cycle are organized around changes in the lives of her husband, children, or parents. Accompanying ritual communication reinforces her role as caretaker and nurturer, but may say little about the meaning of her life. For example, maturation or puberty rites are either demeaning or nonexistent. The onset of menstruation is often experienced as a secretive and in some ways shameful or even "dirty" occurrence. Leaving home for women on all socioeconomic levels has in the past been marked usually by marriage, the bridewealth idea in our society carried through in the tradition of the bride's family "paying" to see her married. No widely sanctioned rituals exist to mark the passage from home to public life for women for whom marriage is not the major leaving home marker.

No well-defined, culturally sanctioned childbirth ritual exists in our society that helps a woman incorporate the difficult role of "mother." The expectant mother is given a "shower," a rite whereby she receives gifts for the infant. After the birth she may participate contingently in a christening or, traditionally, in the case of the bris, may be excluded altogether. These rites welcome the child but do not define or celebrate motherhood. Furthermore, in our mobile, urban society, unlike in most folk societies, women often have been cut off from the support of other women during childbirth. We can speculate, here, that there may be a relationship between postpartum depression and the lack of adequate social validation and support through ritual of this major transition. Women are beginning to reclaim childbirth rituals. Not only is the midwife (and nurse practitioner) returning in increasing numbers, but some women are birthing in more natural and comfortable settings, often with the participation of family members and friends. The LaMaze program, which prepares both men and women for birthing and parenting in an organized, orderly fashion, may be thought of as a contemporary birth ritual.

From marriage on, many of the central rites of passage in which women participate, if she is a mother, are related to the movement through the life cycle of her children: their birthdays, graduations, and marriages. Later she may become the central caretaker for her parents, as they age and die. It is not clear, if transition rituals are so focused on the needs of others, how the changes, separations, and redefinitions a woman faces are mastered or incorporated. Finally, if a woman does not follow the traditional life course and is unconnected to husband or children, her life may lack recognizable markers, leaving her forever on the margins or in what Turner (1969) might define as a "liminal" phase.

## WOMEN, RITUAL, AND FAMILY THERAPY

Ritual and therapy have much in common. Understanding and planned use of ritual power adds a vital dimension to therapeutic work. An examination of the form of therapy reveals that it shares many of the characteristics of ritual and, indeed, may be considered a ritual. It is repetitive, occurring usually at the same place and time. In fact its ritualized character is demonstrated by the resistance both therapist and client experience when a change in place or time is made. Much of the communication and action is ritualized, including prescribed forms of beginnings and endings and clearly delineated behaviors and roles for the actors in the drama.

Further, therapy, like ritual, takes place in time "out of time," in a space marked off from the territory of everyday life, where a different set of norms and forms apply. In that sense, the therapeutic experience, like many rituals, has a liminal quality; it is neither here nor there, suspended in time and space. Thus, if we follow the ritual analogy, therapy offers a sacred and a dangerous opportunity for confirmation or change.

It is, perhaps, therapy's ritual character that provides it with so much power. But does this elevate the therapist to the powerful and mysterious role of shaman? Does this heightened authority place the therapist beyond question or reproach? What are the implicit messages about the relative power and status of client and therapist, particularly if the therapist is a man and the client a woman? The first question a gender sensitive therapist should ask is "What is the impact of the ritualized aspects of my therapeutic method or style? Is it demeaning or dignifying and empowering, does it enact a hierarchical and dominant relationship or an egalitarian one?"

Individual and family difficulties are likely to occur at key transition points in the life cycle or after such points because a transition has not been fully accomplished. Traditionally, rituals that enact and express rites of passage (Van Gennep, 1909) have marked and facilitated such transitions. Haley (1973) has suggested, at least in the case of the young adult leaving home, that family therapy itself can serve as a leaving home ritual, ushering the participants through the steps to the new status and providing the young person with a sustaining or mentoring relationship throughout the liminal phase, a period during which he or she has left the old and not yet taken on the new. Haley warns that the ritual of therapy may also be used to forestall or obviate change, as in long-term therapy with a discontented and anomic woman, which may itself repeatedly confirm that the problem lies within the person rather than in the situation (Haley, 1973).

The form of therapy itself, then, holds ritual power. Therapy may also focus on the rituals or potential for rituals in the life of the client as an arena and opportunity for change. The gender-sensitive therapist can help a woman reclaim and enrich her ritual life, in the process defining or redefining herself and her relationships, completing transitions, and altering the ways she wishes to participate in her domestic and public worlds. "Leaving home" cases provide such an example. Too often, family therapists, following cultural norms which define women as contingent, frame their goals in terms of helping the young adult to leave home or to differentiate from his or her parents (usually from mother). How often does the therapist work with the mother to develop a ritual or series of rituals that facilitate her transition to an "empty nest," to perhaps a changed balance between domestic and public life, to a redefinition of self and an integration of a new status? Family therapists need to help women claim their own experiences and to move through family transitions not as passive observers or as best supporting actresses to the stars of the drama, but as active participants, shaping and expressing themselves and their realities. Thus therapists can help women to become, in Myerhoff's (1983) words, the authors of themselves. A few examples will illustrate.

What rituals exist in our society for the female's transition from childhood to adolescence to adulthood? For many young girls, the first pelvic examination, an often demeaning and even terrifying experience, serves as the modern version of a traditional puberty rite. What messages does such an experience, usually at the hands of a male doctor (shaman) communicate? The onset of menstruation is another dramatic and memorable event which marks coming physical maturity. Responses of those around her (for example, joking, secrecy, lessons in cleanliness) may stimulate a sense of embarrassment and shame, communicating to the young girl powerful negative messages about the meaning of being a woman. Other rituals may be less negative but may offer insufficient or irrelevant definitional material for the times. For example, the "sweet sixteen" party or the *bat mitzvah* (themselves not without their ironic elements) may serve for some girls as adulthood markers. For many others, however, it is more likely that, until a wedding, "growing up" for the young woman is never marked or celebrated, perhaps because women are not defined as adults separate from family until they marry. Therapists can help families devise rituals that express the family's beliefs and values and help their female members move through the life cycle according to those meanings.

For example, the onset of menstruation can be welcomed in a way which celebrates the girl's coming maturity. Several families in our practice have planned celebratory dinners, marking the event with open discussions about the meaning of menstruation and the girl's new potential for creating life. Some families have included small gifts, perhaps a family heirloom that passes through women, down the generations. Other families have designed all-female initiation ceremonies in which, for example, mother, grandmother, and sister participate in helping the young girl to say goodbye to childhood and to anticipate both the joys and responsibilities that come with sexual maturity. Puberty rites which mark the beginning of fertility may help to undo the denial that is often a factor in early adolescent pregnancy.

Maturation and differentiation from the family of course take place over a long period of time, and the absence of a marker such as marriage may leave a young woman in a prolonged adolescent-like or liminal status. The family therapist can help the woman and her family enact her adulthood and her independence. For example, some families in our practice have designed "apartment showers" or "independence parties" which announce and celebrate the fact that the young woman now has her own home. She may be helped to plan a dinner on her own turf for her family or, even more dramatically, to hostess her first family holiday dinner. Other families have devised rituals to mark a young woman's starting her first job. As men are generally in charge of the outside world, the father's participation and "permission" in such a ritual is important. Rituals such as these help the young woman "leave home."

Particularly underritualized and undefined is the life cycle of the woman who never marries. Parents, married siblings, and the young woman herself may believe that the unmarried daughter of the family should take major responsibility for the maintenance and support of parents or other family members around ritual events. Her other commitments and the demands on her time and energy may not be valued since she "has no family of her own." A major therapeutic strategy in work with the overburdened and often highly resentful single woman, alone or in extended family interviews, involves helping all concerned better distribute the caretaking roles. One client was helped to develop, circulate, and then evaluate the impact of a very clear and poignant "resignation" letter, as she redefined her "job" in the family. Another developed a series of family meetings, during which she was able to communicate to her siblings and parents the meanings of her own life, relationships, and commitments and the family was able to develop new ways of sharing family responsibilities. In the following example, neither the client nor her family validates the fact that she has formed a new family:

Marilyn, who has lived with Linda in a lesbian relationship for 25 years, was angrily and passively defined as caretaker of her aged mother, who lived in a retirement home at some distance from the couple. Marilyn's brother, married with children and grandchildren, although he lived much closer to the mother and had always been described as the mother's "favorite," took little responsibility. The organization of the family was particularly obvious in the rituals around Christmas. The celebration was held at the brother's home. Although Marilyn had always been welcome at the homes of Linda's family of origin, her family, although "civil" to Linda, had never included her in the family rituals, explaining to Marilyn that "it was too crowded." Marilyn, who had never felt approved of and was afraid to proclaim her own "marriage," had not been able to challenge this rule which, understandably, stimulated much conflict in the couple's relationship. Marilyn's job was to pick up and return mother to her home, and to dutifully enact the roles of helpful daughter, sister, aunt, and great aunt during these times; roles she performed with resentment and reluctance. When asked why she didn't spend Christmas with Linda, Marilyn would respond, "I have to pick up Mother and take her to my brother's."

In this situation, the therapist helped Marilyn explore the meanings for her life of the old family rituals and to devise strategies to express her separateness and adulthood in relation to her family of origin. One strategy involved the refashioning of the Christmas and other holiday rituals that made them more flexible and more expressive of her couple status, allowing the couple to spend time together, independent times with their respective families, and time as a couple with each of their families, in their home as well as in the homes of relatives. The lesbian theme proved to be somewhat of a red herring; although Marilyn thought that her family believed and the family had implied that this was an unacceptable life choice, the more fundamental issue was one of leaving home at the age of 54, of announcing to her family that she had a life of her own with meaning and value.

There have been many definitions of family in our culture. The most accurate may be "a family is the people you spend the major holidays with."

In this age of rapidly changing and varied lifestyles and family forms, some important events or transitions in the lives of both men and women may be underritualized because there are no traditional rituals to call upon. For example, although we ritualize marriage, we fail to ritualize an equally important event, divorce. Women whose self-definitions are heavily tied to their roles as wives may have particular difficulty in incorporating the new status of "single" or "divorcee." Part of the therapeutic work may involve the designing of a ritual that enacts the relinquishing of the old relationship and the incorporation of the new. One client, for example, some months after the initial separation, invited her husband out to dinner. Together they reminisced about some of their positive and important times together, sharing new insights, each "giving" to the other something to take away. This same woman also planned a party to celebrate the granting of the divorce, as well as a time with her own family to discuss the implications of her new status as single woman and to participate in the family's mourning of the lost son-in-law.

It is possible, in like manner, to help women and families to construct rituals that facilitate any new transition throughout a woman's life cycle, or enable her to complete an earlier, incomplete transition. Other women may need help in freeing themselves from rigid and demeaning daily ritual patterns (Selvini-Palazzoli et al., 1977; van der Hart, 1983), in resolving old, unfinished issues, or in completing the mourning of earlier losses. The therapist must not only be knowledgeable concerning ritual form and aware of subtle gender and power issues, but must be most sensitive to the family's style, its metaphors, its symbols, its ethnicity, its realm of possibility in designing rituals. The ritual will "work" only if it emerges from their culture and expresses their meanings; the ritual imposes change but the therapist cannot impose a ritual out of context. The following illustrates the use of a ritual assignment in the resolution of a conflicted father-daughter relationship.

> Joanne, a 40-year-old professional woman, had been the favorite daughter and "girl Friday" for her father, a distinguished psychiatrist. Her father died when she was 22-years-old and, unable to challenge his power or authority while he was still alive, was having difficulty claiming the leadership roles for which she clearly had potential. A simple ritual was prescribed. Joanne was to visit her father's grave twice a week for exactly 30 minutes. She could remain silent, or she could say whatever she wanted to say to her father. Although she reported that she felt self-conscious and awkward during the

first such trip, before long she was talking to her father. After several such visits she began to express, with considerable anger, her resentment about his control and domination and her fear of him and of his criticism. Not long after, Joanne accepted a challenging and exciting administrative position.

## THE RITUALS OF EVERYDAY LIFE

Daily rituals may lock a woman into subservient roles, they may demean or undervalue her, or they may orchestrate an egalitarian, collaborative family style with dignity and flexibility in terms of available roles. This objectification of the meaning system through the study of ritual gives a woman, a marital pair, or a family the opportunity to evaluate these meanings and, if they wish, to change them through the restructuring of the daily rituals. The key questions to ask in such an examination are: What does the ritual say about the actors? What does it say about women and women's roles? Does it characterize women as second class, dependent, competent only in household and nurturing tasks and incompetent in the outer world, in dealing with money, or mechanical things?

Women and families can be helped to refashion their daily rituals to express a different vision. For example, many couples seen in therapy in which an angry or depressed wife expresses ambiguous dissatisfaction, are locked into struggles about gender role, gender equality, and division of labor. Although the wife may be working outside of the home while the husband "helps" around the house, an exploration of the family's ritual life may reveal that the wife's domestic workload is much heavier than any other family member. She may be trapped in but unable to grasp cognitively the fact that she participates in a traditional and subservient role in a new context in which self-expectations and those of her family for her are unrealistic. Both partners may wish to change but experience themselves as helpless, partly because the old rituals are so powerful. In such situations, clients can be encouraged to take control of their daily rituals, to refashion them to express how they wish to participate in a changing world and a changing marital relationship.

The most powerful and memorable family rituals usually are tied to holidays. Holiday rituals communicate most dramatically the family's world view and also provide a valuable opportunity for change in the roles and structure of the family. Rituals that redistribute the work and ceremonial tasks involved in holidays provide obvious opportunities for redefinition. Holiday time also heightens the meaning of other kinds of rituals, as in the following example:

> Sarah came for help several months following the death of her mother, with whom she had had a close and companionable relationship. She was depressed and angry, and felt isolated in her grief as her husband and two sons who were feeling the loss in their own ways avoided the subject. Her husband refused to accompany her for help. Supported by her therapist and in fear and trembling, she prepared a prayer which she read at Christmas dinner. This ritual evoked the memory of her mother, marked that this was the first Christmas they had spent without her, and expressed the loss the family had experienced. Her older son, close to tears, ran angrily from the room, while her husband scowled. Later that afternoon, as a continuing part of the ritualized remembrance, she set up the movie projector (not something she usually did), and watched home movies in which the grandmother had played a central part. One by one, her family joined her and an hour of sharing and reminiscing ensued.

## WOMEN AND PUBLIC LIFE

When we turn to women's lives in the public world, where women are challenging both the power structure and old stereotypes, there is no blueprint and considerable creativity is demanded. As a woman moves into corporate and other public arenas, her role often assumes a domestic quality, at least symbolically. She may make the coffee in the office, remind her male colleagues not to forget an important meeting, take the minutes, or in other ways perform roles that "serve" men. In working with women in public life, and in our own professional lives, we must become more aware of the subtle ways women are defined or even demeaned. Men understandably do not wish to relinquish their symbols of power and authority.

As women family therapists, we have in the past sometimes hung back in making our claims on the ritual lives of our professions. We continue to support conferences which feature a token woman speaker, we tolerate the addressing of a woman on the dais by her first name while men are addressed by their titles, and we remain silent when women are publicly attacked or humiliated. We have, for the most part, enacted our domestic roles in our professional rituals, staying in our place. It may be that until women in the mental health professions claim their share of the ritual lives of their professions and devise and enact rituals which define, express, and celebrate women's perspectives and roles, we will be unable to help our working women clients claim their public ritual lives.

## CONCLUSION

Ritual offers family therapists a powerful mode in helping women to master life transitions, alter relationships, and construct more meaningful self-definitions. Family therapy is itself a ritual which possesses considerable power in reinforcing or changing particular family roles and relationships; therefore, family therapists need to be knowledgeable concerning the form and content of ritual and sensitive to the impact of the therapeutic ritual on women and on family life. In this article we have suggested a number of ways that ritual impacts the lives of women as well as ways therapists may help women reclaim their ritual lives.

## NOTES

1. For Levi-Strauss (1969) the essence of kinship systems lies in the exchange of women by men. For a fascinating discussion of his theory, see Rubin (1975).

2. We thank Norma Diamond, Professor of Anthropology at the University of Michigan, for this idea.

## REFERENCES

Bamberger, J. (1974). The Myth of Matriarchy: Why Men Rule in Primitive Society. In M. Rosaldo & L. Lamphere (Eds.), *Women, Culture, and Society*. Stanford, CA: Stanford University Press.

Caplow, T. et al. (1982). *Middletown Families: Fifty Years of Change and Continuity*. Minneapolis: University of Minnesota Press.

Douglas, M. (1966). *Purity and Danger: An Analysis of Concepts of Pollution and Taboo*. New York: Praeger.

Friedman, E. (1980). Systems and Ceremonies: A Family View of Rites of Passage. In E.A. Carter & M. McGoldrick (Eds.), *The Family Life Cycle: A Framework for Family Therapy*. New York: Gardner Press.

Gennep, A. van. (1909). *Les Rites de Passage*. Paris: Libraire Critique, Emil Mourry.

Gluck, N., Dannefer, E., and Milea, K. (1980). Women in Families. In E. A.

Carter and M. McGoldrick (Eds.), *The Family Life Cycle: A Framework for Family Therapy*. New York: Gardner Press.

Haley, Jay. (1973). *Uncommon Therapy*. New York: W.W. Norton.

Hart, O. van der. (1983). *Rituals in Psychotherapy: Transition and Continuity*. New York: Irvington.

Levi-Strauss, C. (1969). *The Elementary Structures of Kinship*. Boston: Beacon Press.

Moore, S. & Myerhoff, B. (1977). Introduction: Secular Ritual: Forms and Meanings. In S. Moore & B. Myerhoff (Eds.), *Secular Ritual*. Amsterdam, The Netherlands: Van Gorcum.

Myerhoff, B. (1978). *Number Our Days*. New York: Simon and Schuster.

Myerhoff, B. (1983). Rites of Passage. Plenary speech, National Symposium, National Association of Social Workers, Washington, D.C., November.

Ortner, S. (1974). Is Female to Male as Nature Is to Culture? In M. Rosaldo & L. Lamphere (Eds.), *Woman, Culture, and Society*. Stanford, CA: Stanford University Press.

Rappaport, R. (1979). The Obvious Aspects of Ritual. In R. Rappoport, *Ecology, Meaning, and Religion*. Richmond, CA: North Atlantic Books.

Reiss, D. (1981). *The Family's Construction of Reality*. Cambridge, MA: Harvard University Press.

Rich, A. (1976). *Of Woman Born: Motherhood as Experience and Institution*. New York: Bantam Books.

Rubin, G. (1975). The Traffic in Women: Notes on the "Political Economy" of Sex. In R. Reiter (Ed.), *Toward an Anthropology of Women*. New York: Monthly Review Press.

Russo, N. (1978). Beyond Adolescence: Some Suggested New Directions for Study of Female Development in the Middle and Later Years. In J. Sherman & F. Denmark (Eds.), *The Psychology of Women: Future Directions in Research*. New York: Psychological Dimensions, Inc.

Selvini-Palazzoli, M. et al., Family rituals: A powerful tool in family therapy. *Family Process*, 16, 445-543.

Turner, V. (1969). *The Ritual Process: Structure and Anti-Structure*. Ithaca: Cornell University Press.

Wolin, S. & Bennett, L. (1984). Family Rituals. *Family Process* 23, 401-420.

# Teaching an Integrated Model
# of Family Therapy:
# Women as Students,
# Women as Supervisors

Marianne Ault-Riché

**SUMMARY.** This paper describes the use of an apprenticeship model of supervision in the context of a feminist-informed, Integrated Model of Family Therapy. This therapeutic model proposes a continuum of emphasis upon gender issues, ranging from their explicit handling in cases where they are presented as problematic by the couple themselves to an implicit handling of gender issues through metaphor. Case examples are presented to illustrate this continuum as well as to illustrate typical scenarios for women as students and as supervisors. The former scenarios are discussed in terms of (1) knowledge base, (2) assertiveness, (3) fear of men's power, and (4) sex-role stereotypes. The latter scenarios are discussed in terms of (1) sexist biases, (2) women's role in the institution, (3) attitudes toward women in authority, and (4) sex-role expectations.

"Challenges and Promises of Training Women as Family Systems Therapists" by Caust, Libow, and Raskin appeared in *Family Process* in 1981. Its publication marked the beginning of a wide-

Marianne Ault-Riché, MSW, is Curriculum Coordinator, Marriage and Family Therapy Training Program, The Menninger Foundation, Box 829, Topeka, KS 66601.

spread effort to reconcile feminism and systems theory in family therapy training (Libow, Raskin & Caust, 1982). In the seven years between Hare-Mustin's 1978 challenge to the field, "A Feminist Approach to Family Therapy" and Goldner's comprehensive overview, "Feminism and Family Therapy" in 1985, there has been a proliferation of presentations concerning "women's issues." Now that the major theoretical and political ideas have been addressed, attention is turning to their application in practice and supervision. The present paper builds upon the work of Libow (1986) and Ault-Riché (1986) as well as upon the earlier work of Caust, Libow, and Raskin (1981).[1]

A discussion of family therapy training necessarily concerns what is taught, to whom, by whom and how. This paper proposes (1) a feminist-informed Integrated Model of Family Therapy with a "continuum of emphasis" upon gender issues, (2) describes an apprenticeship model of supervision, and (3) addresses special issues for women as students and as supervisors.[2]

In order to propose a gender-sensitive approach to family therapy, one must begin with a definition of therapy itself. Distinguished family therapists who identify themselves as feminists can be found in all the major "camps" of family therapy: Structural, Strategic, Interactional, Systemic, Multigenerational, Behavioral, and Object-Relations. Each of these schools defines therapy somewhat differently and each can be critiqued from a feminist perspective (Ault-Riché 1986; Avis, 1985; Jacobson, 1983; Margolin et al., 1983). It appears that within each of the major schools, feminists are attempting to delineate gender-sensitive applications of their theories and techniques (Pinderhughes, 1986; Roth & Murphy, 1986). Wheeler and Avis formerly of Purdue University are currently attempting to define the parameters of such approaches by studying feminists who are family therapy teachers. The author predicts that although the Purdue research will clearly indicate the relevant theoretical issues and values, it will be less clear regarding clinical applications due to the wide range of ways in which therapy itself is defined.

## A "CONTINUUM OF EMPHASIS" UPON GENDER ISSUES

In the Integrated Model of Family Therapy from which I practice, therapy is defined as the provision of cognitive, affective, and behavioral experiences which increase the options of clients (Ault-Riché & Rosenthal, 1986; Ault-Riché & Rosenthal, in press.) This model reflects a synthesis of seven major schools of family therapy, is gender-sensitive in that it acknowledges the feminist critique of family therapies, and proposes a "continuum of emphasis" upon gender issues in clinical practice. *This continuum ranges from the explicit handling of gender issues in cases where these are presented as problematic by the couple themselves, to an implicit handling of these issues through metaphor. The general goal of therapy, however, is to expand clients' options and not to impose upon them social arrangements the therapist finds aesthetically or politically pleasing.*

A "feminist-informed" approach to family therapy may be said to be predicated upon certain assumptions: (1) the personal is political: the family is embedded in a socioeconomic context which is both patriarchal and misogynist; (2) to not deal with the sexism in our clients' lives is to endorse and perpetuate the existing oppressive social arrangements; and (3) there is no value-free therapy. The precise ways in which the therapist acts upon these assumptions, however, is best determined by "where the client is at." The art of therapy lies in facilitating the client's movement from "where she is at," to considering where she might be, to setting foot on the path of her choice. The art of therapy is after all a rhetorical art — a healing with words — persuading the client to look at things differently. The experienced therapist chooses her words wisely and moves incrementally, taking her cue from the client. Movement along the continuum can be described in terms of the therapist's management of timing, zeal, and metaphor.

When a couple presents for therapy identifying a gender-related power imbalance as the problem itself, the therapist can proceed with explicit sex role analysis, assertiveness training, and problem-solving. She can directly educate the couple about male and female socialization, helping them to understand their behavior in context. Typically it is the woman who wants change (e.g., husband to share household tasks and express feelings) and the man who wants the status quo or a return to the original (traditional) marital contract. In such situations the therapist does well to proceed cautiously though explicitly because, as Goodrich (1984) points out, the evangelical mode may not be particularly useful. Moreover, as Lerner warns, "it is not therapeutic to attempt to 'liberate' a patient from cultural sex-role stereotypes if that patient relies on them to shore up and maintain a shaky sense of gender identity" (Lerner, 1978).

A second type of self presentation is that of the couple whose power imbalance is obviously gender-related but is not identified as such by the clients themselves, e.g., wife abuse and exploitation of a "supermother." In the former situation, the therapist can often afford to be quite explicit because she is working with the power of the law behind her. The therapist may draw upon a variety of interventions, including sex role analysis, education about socialization, and exposing the complementarity of women's conditioned selflessness with society's prescription for male violence. However, although the therapy may be court mandated, the clients are usually free to choose their treater. A too zealous therapist, therefore, may find her effectiveness if not her caseload reduced. Again, as Goodrich (1984) points out, clients at an early stage developmentally may find a raised consciousness terrifying rather than liberating. On the other hand, clients in abusive situations may be more open to unfamiliar if not radical gender-related formulations if they view their situation as abnormal. "How do I understand this situation which I never dreamed I would find myself in?" For those women who have denied or inhibited their anger, it may be useful to universalize their experience by describing the ubiquitous social prohibitions against the expression of female anger. Likewise are there strong social injunctions against rebelling from a primarily service-oriented role and submissive stance vis-a-vis men. Anger is thus redirected against the self, other women and children, or vented in impotent fashion. Moreover, the energy bound in suppressing, inhibiting, and redirecting anger makes it unavailable for creative pursuits (Bernardez-Bonesatti, 1978).

Couples in this second group (i.e., with obviously gender-related problems not explicitly presented as such) require a therapist who can confront without blaming, support without overidentifying, be angry without punishing, and be political without being overbearing. This middle ground in the "continuum of emphasis" upon gender issues is one in which the therapist flexibly shifts between explicit and implicit work on power issues between the couple as well as between the clients and herself. The therapist here is neither primarily self-disclosing (giving vent to her own opinions and outrage), nor exclusively, elusively strategic. Both her theoretical understanding and her therapeutic use of power are contextual. Stierlin (1983) reflecting upon the issue of family therapy as a science or an art suggests:

Today I am more convinced than I ever was that striving for power, control and definition of relationships is a—perhaps *the*—central aspect of our human and family nature . . . And as this is the case I feel that a major part of the art of family therapy must be seen in the recognition of these power games in all their subtlety and the development of counterstrategies that enable the therapist to intervene effectively in these games. But—and this is where Bateson's position comes into its own—artistry in understanding interpersonal power games and devising counterstrategies is not enough. Participation and countering on the part of the therapist can have a genuinely therapeutic effect only if the therapist also recognizes power as a corrupting metaphor . . . if his attitude toward power is determined by curiosity in the sense in which Bateson used the word; insight into the necessary imperfection of all our knowledge; humility as an antidote for hubris; empathy in the last resort, *wisdom*. (p. 422)

At one end of the "continuum of emphasis" upon gender issues are those couples in which one or both presents their power imbalance as a problem. With these, the therapist works explicitly. In the middle of the continuum are those who do not initially identify their problems as gender-related but at least one of them is open to this view. At the far end of the "continuum of emphasis" are those clients whose presenting problems are less dramatically related to gender issues and whose values are quite conservative. For example, the child of a couple with a traditional marriage is presented as a bedwetter; the husband works two jobs and the wife, a homemaker, is mildly depressed. Although the therapist can easily formulate the family's problem from a feminist perspective, the couple has traditional values, firmly held, and requests only that the child stop wetting. The therapist who possesses the skills to stop the bedwetting without directly addressing the gender issues has several choices: (1) she can view the therapy only as a symptom-focused consumer service; (2) she can sell the family on an expanded contract which includes gender issues; and (3) she can work in metaphor to create alternative realities and options. A therapist working at the latter end of the "continuum of emphasis" works indirectly and in a very disciplined fashion.

## Case Example

A small-town couple in their mid-40s brought their only child, a 6-year-old hyperactive and intellectually limited boy for family therapy at the recommendation of the school. The presenting problems were short attention span, public masturbation, and cruelty to animals. The father said of his wife in the intake session, "they told me Jolene was retarded, but I married her anyway." Jolene presented as a timid, insecure woman of low average ability. She had not attended any school conferences regarding her son because her husband conveyed to her that she was not capable of so doing. Her parents-in-law were openly critical of her and her father-in-law had once struck her when she had spanked his grandson. Her husband had witnessed this event without interfering.

Family therapy began with an assignment to get baseline data regarding attention span and masturbation. The mother was asked to read to the boy in the interval between his return from school and her dinner preparation. Father, during this time, was finishing up his day's work in the garage. The mother was not to make any effort to force the boy to listen to the stories, and was to keep track of the time he spontaneously attended to her. At the second session the mother reported that he had listened to stories between 30 and 45 minutes each evening and that she had discovered that on the days she read to him he did not masturbate. The therapist praised the mother for her success and assigned her to go to the school to teach the teacher how to keep the boy focused on an interesting activity so that he would not masturbate out of boredom or loneliness.

The therapist thus began to shift the power balance in the parental relationship metaphorically, as an explicit discussion of the gender issues would surely have led to premature termination.

At the metaphorical end of the continuum, fully realizing that there is no value-free therapy, the therapist proceeds indirectly. *She must thus be guided by a therapeutic mandate to work within whatever explicit contract she has forged with the family. This contract is created by her artistry and serves as the ethical safeguard for both the family and herself.*

Training therapists in this Integrated Model is something of a challenge because the model allows for a wide range of goals and thus a wide range of therapist behaviors. This challenge is all the greater when I am training students who rigidly adhere to sex-role stereotypes because of their conditioned limitations.

## THE APPRENTICESHIP MODEL

The Integrated Model from which I practice permits the therapist to contract with the client(s) for goals ranging along a continuum from symptom-relief to problem-solving to long-term work on differentiation of self (Ault-Riché and Rosenthal, in press). This model likewise proposes a "continuum of emphasis" upon gender issues ranging from explicit sex-role analysis to metaphorical interventions. The form of supervision used is also based upon a continuum: the trainee moves from an observer, to a live-supervised member of a family therapy team, to an independent practitioner with consultation available as needed. This training model is based in part upon my experience as a practicum student of Stephen Greenstein's at the Philadelphia Child Guidance Clinic in 1977. It is probably also based in part upon a paternal family history of young people apprenticing as chefs. Unlike some feminists who equate hierarchial arrangements with the excesses of masculine power, I consider executive ability and a comfortable acknowledgement of experience and expertise as attributes of a healthy adult. I furthermore eschew the common practice of thrusting inexperienced therapists without benefit of live supervision upon the poor and the unsophisticated.

Because the apprenticeship model is predicated upon the teacher being clearly in a position of authority, predictable transference phenomena arise in clinical supervision. These will be discussed in terms of typical scenarios for women as students and women as supervisors.

## WOMEN AS STUDENTS

Typical scenarios for women as students will be discussed in terms of four issues: (1) knowledge base, (2) assertiveness, (3) fear of men's power, and (4) sex-role expectations.

### Knowledge Base

Students of family therapy need to be knowledgeable about women's physiology and psychology. There is now a growing body of literature collectively referred to as the new psychology of women which includes such information as the latest thinking about women's adult development, sex-role socialization, mothering world-view, morality, etc. (Ault-Riché, 1986; Libow, 1982).

In my experience, trainees particularly need to be familiar with: (1) typical problems women have communicating and the ubiquitous dread of women's anger (Lerner, 1985); (2) the socioeconomic history of the nuclear American family (Goldner, 1985); (3) adaptive and pathogenic aspects of sex-role stereotypes (Feldman, 1982, 1985; Lerner, 1985; McGoldrick et al., 1982); and (4) the facts about divorce and its differential effects for men and women (Carter & McGoldrick, 1980; Mills, 1984).

*Case example.* A young therapist enthusiastically supported her client's plan to walk out on a philandering husband. The client was being ignored and disrespected by her husband but not sexually or physically abused. The trainee was helped in supervision to acknowledge the client's economic situation and to help her prepare financially as well as psychologically for divorce. A realistic appraisal of the client's limited job skills permitted the therapist to temper her zeal in supporting the client to divorce immediately. The client was thus able to secure placement in a vocational training program and find a housemate before separating from her husband.

### Assertiveness

One of the initial challenges of family systems work, particularly for female trainees is the ability to function flexibly in an authoritative, instrumental "take charge" manner (Caust, Libow & Raskin, 1981). Many women find it stressful, alien, unfeminine, or frightening to actively control the movement in a family unit, given their own socialization in submissive and/or approval-seeking behavior (Libow, 1986). Female trainees often prefer the relationship-oriented aspects of therapy to instrumental tasks which necessitate assertiveness and risk taking. This shift is particularly difficult for students (male or female) trained in psychoanalytic or humanist approaches. Students trained in behavioral approaches often have the opposite problem.

*Case example.* A soft-spoken trainee was directed by her supervisor to get her client to take a firm stand with the client's unruly and disrespectful teenager. The trainee first spoke to the mother as if she were offering her a cup of tea. She next implored her to take action. When this was not effective, the trainee began repeating herself in a rigid voice, berating the teenager with psychodynamic interpretations. In a subsequent session with the supervisor, the trainee was able to acknowledge her difficulty in (1) seeing the mother as *entitled* to respect and (2) using her own strength to model firmness and caring *simultaneously*. This trainee was also told not to say "thank you for coming" at the close of her interviews which seemed to imply that the clients were doing her a favor by showing up at all.

Bernardez-Bonesatti (1978) writes:

> Women are in dire need of reassurance about their destructiveness. It is not verbal reassurance that is needed but the experience in the here and now of one's own legitimate anger in the presence of tolerant and unfrightened witnesses. What women want is a legitimate voice of protest and the flexible ability to yield as well as resist and fight. To preserve the caring and nurturing aspects of women while gaining the freedom to be active and aggressive and the right to express anger requires several steps, among the first one the demythologizing of woman's destructiveness.

> For assertiveness to exist, freedom from fear of disapproval by others and of one's own destructiveness is in order. An assertive person stands affirmatively behind her position but not rigidly. Care and respect for others exist side by side with an ability to defend one's rights without guilt and imposition. (p. 218)

## Fear of Men's Power

Libow (1986) writes of the importance of specific skills training for female trainees: the use of nonverbal behaviors to express authority and confidence; the strategic use of voice, language, and posture; the active manipulation of seating arrangements; and the control of communication flow. It is at times unreasonable, however, to expect a trainee to deal with the intimidating power of male clients. At these times the student can learn best from the modeling provided by her supervisor. Afterwards, the student's patterned ways of moving in response to frightening or irrational men can be addressed.

*Case example.* A young child psychiatrist went to the waiting room to meet a new family. She was accompanied by her supervisor, who typically was introduced briefly, before the trainee would explain the videotaping procedure and obtain necessary releases.

Usually the supervisor would at this point withdraw to the observation room. At the mention of videotape, however, the stepfather, who had been pacing about, started shouting obscenely in front of others in the waiting room. He said he was tired of all these therapists telling him what to do and treating him like a guinea pig. He especially hated the male social worker at the State Hospital who had made the referral for family therapy and threatened to go back and "run that guy's dick into the ground." The supervisor directed the man and his family to the interview room while maintaining eye contact with him and repeating that videotaping would not be necessary. Upon entering the interview room the man stood on a chair and attempted to grab the microphone out of the ceiling, shouting that he did not trust these bastards. The supervisor firmly said that the microphone was off, but that it was quite alright to move to a room which did not have a mike in it at all. The man talked incessantly and irrationally with the supervisor calmly repeating and tracking everything he said about his suspicions of and dissatisfactions with previous treaters. Eventually the man settled down and it was determined that he had been sent away to an institution when he was the same age as the identified patient. Having been willing to accommodate to modify the external structure, the supervisor facilitated the structuring of the interview itself, repeatedly acknowledging the man's boundaries, rights, and preferences. She confirmed that she would be present in all interviews working with the child psychiatrist as a family therapy team. Several sessions later the man offered an apology for his behavior and eventually referred to the team with some affection as "the doctor and the gray-haired lady."

### Sex-Role Expectations

Female trainees must regularly deal with the sex-role expectations placed upon them by clients, supervisors, agency administrators, and society at large. In a feminist critique of Functional Family Therapy, Avis (1985) describes how women are expected to be sexual and emotional service stations for men and children: ". . . their exploitation involves systematic socialization which prepares them for unpaid domestic labor, exclusion from the mainstream of economic and political life, and surrender of self-development and self-interest in favor of serving others" (p. 130). As therapists, women are often expected by clients to be nondirective and empathic.

*Case example.* A couple hospitalized their adolescent son after five years of outpatient marital and family therapy did not resolve the presenting problems. Previously each parent had undergone a personal analysis. In the second session the inpatient family therapist attempted to delineate the parents' goals for their son and themselves in operational terms. The therapist asked clarifying questions and sought to keep the dialogue focused. The parents then expressed considerable displeasure with the therapist for not being more interested in their associations and expressions of feelings. The young therapist felt unkind and unfeminine as well as incompetent. Her supervisor helped her to understand the situation in terms of the family members' expectations that she be supportive and undemanding—a therapeutic stance with which this couple had 12 years of experience! The therapist was then able to take a benevolent but firm stance, containing the parents' aggression as they worked together to forge a contract for treatment.

## WOMEN AS SUPERVISORS

Typical scenarios for women as supervisors will be discussed in terms of four issues: (1) sexist biases, (2) women's role in the institution, (3) attitudes toward women in authority, and (4) sex-role expectations.

### Sexist Biases

Supervisors, although they be women, are not free of sexism. Of the sexist attitudes found to characterize psychotherapy in general (APA Task Force on Sex Bias and Sex-Role Stereotyping, 1975), Margolin (1982) finds family therapists to be particularly vulnerable to the following biases: (1) assuming that remaining in a marriage would result in better adjustment for a woman; (2) demonstrating less interest in, or sensitivity to, a woman's career than to a man's career; (3) perpetuating the belief that childrearing and thus the child's problems are solely the responsibility of the mother; (4) exhibiting a double standard for a wife's versus a husband's affair; and (5) deferring to the husband's needs over those of the wife (p. 798). A recent study by Yoger and Shadish (1982) found that even androgynous females who see themselves as relatively free from sex-role limitations, still behave as therapists in accordance with traditional gender expectations. Other studies (Margolin, 1982; Gurman & Klein, 1981; Hare-Mustin, 1978) likewise conclude that family and marital therapists tend to reinforce stereotyped sex-roles.

I have found several exercises to be useful for both supervisors and students in examining their own biases:

1. Family of Origin Exercises
   A. Compare the functioning of your same sex relatives (beginning with great grandparents if possible) in terms of these dimensions: sibling position, physical and emotional health, cultural/religious/ethnic background, sexual orientation, work inside the home, work outside the home, success/failure in combining work in and out of the home, view of women's role, view of men's role, relationship with partner(s), role in community/public sphere.

   B. Examine family members'
      i. clarity of communication; use of I-positions
      ii. problem-solving skills including conflict resolution
      iii. comfort with assertion, authority, confrontation
      iv. constructive use of anger, power

2. A. What stereotypic sex behaviors/traits do you have?
      i. Which are advantageous to you as a family therapist and why?
      ii. Which are disadvantageous and why?

   B. What unstereotypic sex behaviors/traits do you have?
      i. Which are advantageous to you as a family therapist and why?
      ii. Which are disadvantageous and why?

   C. What is your idea of a healthy adult female? Healthy adult male?

   D. What are you most negatively reactive to in women? In men?

   E. Do you tend to expect more of female or male clients? How do you understand your biases?

   F. Do you tend to fuse/distance, overfunction/underfunction in the company of females/males? How do you understand your patterned ways of moving?

## Women's Role in the Institution

Libow (1986) points out that a woman supervisor may be devalued by her students if she is perceived to be on the fringes of a male institution. Chadbourne (1980) reports that female trainees often avoid female supervisors or mentors because they are not seen as having sufficient power to protect students or open doors for them. The reader is referred to Kanter's work for an understanding of the predictable dynamics in institutions where only a token number of a given population hold positions of power (Kanter, 1982).

## Attitudes Toward Women in Authority

In an essay on the psychodynamic and interactional aspects of women in authority, Bernardez (1983) writes:

> The tendency to devalue women and to deny or ignore their competence has . . . a number of determinants in men: the superiority of the dominant class and/or any member of that class is put into question if the ability and competence of the woman is obvious and leads her to positions of power. Some men react as if they had been humiliated when a woman demonstrates her excellence over them. That is why it is frequent to find among women, the tendency to minimize their abilities and to diminish their visibility . . . The model of female authority is a primitive and irrational one, since it is not just the mother of childhood (and in subsequent years the female teacher) but the idealized and feared image of her that is maintained out of awareness. The scarcity of women leaders in public life and the lack of models of feminine authority in the adult lives of individuals does not permit us to edit and review these early versions of interaction with females in power. (p. 44)

The challenge for a woman supervisor is to act with firm benevolence. In the face of aggression and criticism from subordinates she will do well to protect herself with detachment, neutrality, and objectivity, i.e., to contain the aggression without retaliation, helplessness, or expression of intense affect (Bernardez, 1983).

It is not uncommon for students (usually male) of a supervisor using the apprenticeship model (a directive rather than collegial approach) to engage in discussions of the merits of the model as an avoidance of dealing with their discomfort with an authoritative woman. I have learned the hard way not to accommodate seemingly reasonable requests for collegiality when the students are in the early stages of training. As a supervisor of supervisors, I am currently witnessing the struggles of women colleagues, who, upon becoming supervisors experience intense transference phenomena for the first time. Those supervisors who present as primarily nurturant are devalued for not being clear thinkers; those who present as primarily task-focused are experienced as dangerous. Doehrman's (1976) essay on parallel process in supervision as well as Lerner's popular book *The Dance of Anger* (1985) may be helpful to supervisors in such situations.

### Sex-Role Expectations

Related to the issue of attitudes toward women in authority is that of sex-role expectations in general—expectations held by clients as well as by supervisees. I recall with amusement the time I entered the therapy room after a male trainee was hopelessly failing to communicate with the father of a seriously disturbed boy. The trainee had little knowledge of family therapy, and barely spoke English. The father had complained appropriately and implied that he wanted a different therapist. At this point I entered the room, joined with the father, and obtained a treatment contract. Turning to the male trainee the father said, "You've probably got the brains and she knows how to get it across."

*Case example.* A female social worker, age 32, was assigned to provide family therapy supervision to a male psychiatrist, age 33. In the beginning she clarified the supervisory contract—the apprenticeship model and the live supervision. The trainee's initial struggles with this structure were taken at face value, i.e., as reflections of his unfamiliarity with both the theory and practice of family therapy. For example, a client called the psychiatrist between sessions to get medication for her hyperactive child. He consulted with her at length over the phone and then called in a prescription. In supervision, he was subsequently helped to understand (1) the structural significance of prescribing medication; (2) the metamessage to the family about the workings of the family therapy team; and (3) the ubiquitous experience of physicians training to be therapists who feel safe and competent both in responding to urgent requests and in prescribing. Later on in the learning process, when the supervisor had established herself as authoritative but not destructive or engulfing, she facilitated the trainee's examination of his struggle with the multiple aspects of their hierarchial incongruity in terms of sex-role status, age, and professional degree.

## CONCLUSION

This paper has described the use of an apprenticeship model of supervision in the context of a feminist-informed, Integrated Model of Family Therapy. This therapeutic model proposes a continuum of emphasis upon gender issues, ranging from their explicit handling in cases where they are presented as problematic by the couple themselves, to an implicit handling of gender issues through metaphor. Case examples were presented to illustrate this continuum as well as to illustrate typical scenarios for women as students and as supervisors. The former scenarios were discussed in terms of (1) knowledge base, (2) assertiveness, (3) fear of men's power, and (4) sex-role stereotypes. The latter scenarios were discussed in terms of (1) sexist biases, (2) women's role in the institution, (3) attitudes toward women in authority, and (4) sex-role expectations.

The Integrated Model I teach is predicated upon a practitioner, and thus a supervisor, having a wide behavioral repertoire upon which to draw. She must be firm and benevolent, trustworthy and accountable, disciplined in her spontaneity, and generous of spirit. Stereotypically speaking, she can be both feminine and masculine. As Jung suggests, it helps to be 40.

## NOTES

1. At the time this paper was being typed in final, I discovered a recent paper in this journal by Wheeler et al., (1986), "Rethinking Family Therapy Education and Supervision: A Feminist Model." The reader is referred to this important paper and especially to the three tables presenting perceptual/conceptual and executive skills for (1) developing and maintaining a working alliance, (2) defining the problem, and (3) facilitating change.

2. The author considers herself a feminist and a family therapist but not a feminist family therapist. She hereby apologizes to William Safire for capitulating to the popular misuse of the grammatical term "gender" as a euphemism for "sex."

# REFERENCES

American Psychological Task Force. (1975). Report of the task force on sex bias and sex role stereotyping in psychotherapeutic practice. *American Psychologist, 30*, 1169-1175.

Ault-Riché, M. (Ed.) (1986). *Women and Family Therapy*. Maryland: Aspen Publishing.

Ault-Riché, M. & Rosenthal, D. (1986). Family Therapy with Symptomatic Adolescents: An Integrated Model. In G. Leigh & G. Peterson (Eds.), *Adolescents in Families*. Texas: Southwestern Publishing.

Ault-Riché, M. & Rosenthal, D. (in press). *Family Therapy for a New Age: Seeing Through Techniques and Integrating Models*. New Jersey: Prentice-Hall.

Avis, J. (1985). The politics of functional family therapy: A feminist critique. *Journal of Marital and Family Therapy, 11*, 127-138.

Bernardez, T. (1983). Women in Authority: Psychodynamic and Interactional Aspects. *Group Work with Women/Group Work with Men*. New York: Haworth Press.

Bernardez-Bonesatti, T. (1978). Women and anger: Conflicts with aggression in contemporary women. *Journal of the American Medical Women's Association, 33*, 215-219.

Carter, E. & McGoldrick, M. (Eds.) (1980). *The Family Life Cycle*. New York: Gardner Press.

Caust, B.L., Libow, J.A. & Raskin, P.A. (1981). Challenges and promises of training women as family systems therapists. *Family Process, 20*, 439-447.

Chadbourne, J. (1980). Female to Female Mentoring Relationships. *Proceedings of the Association for Women in Psychiatry,* Seventh Annual National Conference on Feminist Psychology, Los Angeles.

Doehrman, M. (1976). Parallel process in supervision. *Menninger Bulletin, 40*, 3-104.

Feldman, L. (1979). Marital conflict and marital intimacy: An integrative psychodynamic-behavioral-systemic model. *Family Process, 18*, 69-78.

Feldman, L. (1982). Sex Roles and Family Dynamics. In F. Walsh (Ed.), *Normal Family Process*. New York: Guilford Press.

Feldman, L. (1986). Sex-Role Issues in Marital Therapy. In N. Jacobson & A. Gurman (Eds.), *Clinical Handbook of Marital Therapy*. New York: Guilford Press.

Framo, J.L. (1970). Symptoms from a Family Transactional Viewpoint. In N.W. Ackerman, S. Lieb & J.K. Pearce (Eds.), *Family Therapy in Transition*, Boston: Little, Brown.

Goldner, V. (1985). Feminism and family therapy. *Family Process, 24*, 31-47.

Goodrich, T. (1984). Interface and Ideology: Zeal. Symposium conducted at the Women's Institute of the Meeting of the Association of Marriage and Family Therapy, San Francisco.

Gurman, A. (1980). Behavioral marriage therapy in the 1980s: The challenge of integration. *American Journal of Family Therapy, 8*, 86-96.

Gurman, A. & Klein, M. (1981). Women and Behavioral Marriage and Family Therapy: An Unconscious Male Bias? In E.A. Blechman (Ed.), *Contemporary Issues in Behavior Modification With Women*, New York: Guilford Press.

Hare-Mustin, R. (1978). A feminist approach to family therapy. *Family Process, 17*, 181-194.

Jacobson, N. (1983). Beyond empiricism: The politics of marital therapy. *American Journal of Family Therapy, 11*, 11-24.

Kanter, R.M. (1977). Some effects of proportions on group life. *American Journal of Sociology, 82*, 965-990.

Kaplan, H.S. (1979). *Disorders of Sexual Desire.* New York: Simon & Schuster.

Lerner, H.G. (1978). Adaptive and pathogenic aspects of sex role stereotypes: Applications for parenting and psychotherapy. *American Journal of Psychiatry*, 135:1.

Lerner, H.G. (1985). *The Dance of Anger*, New York: Harper & Row.

Libow, J., Raskin, P. & Caust, B. (1982). Feminist and family systems therapy: Are they irreconcilable? *American Journal of Family Therapy, 10*, 3-12.

Libow, J.A. (1986). Training Family Therapists as Feminists. In M. Ault Riché (Ed.), *Women and Family Therapy.* Maryland: Aspen Publishing.

Madanes, C. (1981). *Strategic Family Therapy.* New York: Jossey Bass.

Margolin, G. (1982). Ethical and legal considerations in marital and family therapy. *American Psychologist, 37*, 788-801.

Margolin, G., Talovic, S. & Weinstein, C. (1983). The areas of change questionnaire: A practical approach to marital assessment. *Journal of Counseling and Clinical Psychiatry, 51*, 944-955.

Margolin, G., Talovic, G., Fernandez, V. & Onorato, R. (1983). Sex role considerations and behavioral marital therapy: Equal does not mean identical. *Journal of Marital and Family Therapy, 9*, 131-145.

McGoldrick, M., Pearce, J., & Giordano, J. (Eds.) (1982). *Ethnicity and Family Therapy.* New York: Guilford Press.

Mills, D. (1984). A model for stepfamily development. *Family Relations, 33*, 365-372.

Okun, B.F. (1983). Gender Issues of Family Systems Therapists. In B. Okun & S. Gladding (Eds.), *Issues in Training Marriage and Family Therapists*, ERIC/CAPS Ann Arbor, Michigan.

Penn, P. (1985). Feed forward: Future questions, future maps. *Family Process, 24*, 299-310.

Pinderhughes, E. (1986). Minority Women: A Nodal Position in the Functioning of the Social System. In M. Ault-Riché (Ed.), *Women and Family Therapy*, Maryland: Aspen Publishing.

Pinsof, W. (1983). Integrative problem-centered therapy: Toward the synthesis of family and individual psychotherapies. *Journal of Marital and Family Therapy, 9*, 19-35.

Roth, S. & Murphy, B. (1986). Therapeutic Work with Lesbian Clients: A Systemic Therapy View. In M. Ault-Riché (Ed.), *Women and Family Therapy*, Maryland: Aspen Publishing.

Safire, W. (1984, August). Goodbye Sex, Hello Gender. New York: *New York Times Magazine.*

Sager, C.J. (1976). *Marriage Contracts and Couple Therapy*, New York: Brunner/Mazel.

Schmidt, G. & Trenkle, B. (1985). An Integration of Ericksonian Techniques with Concepts of Family Therapy. In J. Zeig (Ed.), *Erickson Therapy*, Vol. II, New York: Brunner/Mazel.

Stierlin, H. (1983). Family therapy—A science or an art? *Family Process, 22,* 413-423.

Tomm, T. (1985). Circular Interviewing: A Multifaceted Clinical Tool. In D. Campbell & R. Draper (Eds.), *Applications of Systemic Family Therapy: The Milan Method.* New York: Academic Press.

Walters, M. (1985). Notes from an optimistic feminist family therapist. *The Family Therapy Networker, 9*(2), 6.

Wheeler, D. (research in progress). Defining the Parameters of a Feminist or Gender-Sensitive Approach to Family Therapy. Purdue University, Department of Child Development and Family Studies.

Wheeler, D., Avis, J.M., Miller, L.A. & Chaney, C. (1986). Rethinking family therapy education and supervision: A feminist model. *Journal of Psychotherapy & the Family, 1,* 53-72.

Yoger, S. & Shadish, W.R. (1982). A method for monitoring the impact of sex role stereotypes on the therapeutic behavior of beginning psychotherapists. *American Journal of Orthopsychiatry, 52,* 545-548.